FRANKLIN D. ROOSEVELT

Recent Titles in Greenwood Biographies

Langston Hughes: A Biography
Laurie F. Leach

Fidel Castro: A Biography
Thomas M. Leonard

Oprah Winfrey: A Biography
Helen S. Garson

Mark Twain: A Biography
Connie Ann Kirk

Jack Kerouac: A Biography
Michael J. Dittman

Mother Teresa: A Biography
Meg Greene

Jane Addams: A Biography
Robin K. Berson

Rachel Carson: A Biography
Arlene R. Quaratiello

Desmond Tutu: A Biography
Steven D. Gish

Marie Curie: A Biography
Marilyn Bailey Ogilvie

Ralph Nader: A Biography
Patricia Cronin Marcello

Carl Sagan: A Biography
Ray Spangenburg and Kit Moser

Sylvia Plath: A Biography
Connie Ann Kirk

Jesse Jackson: A Biography
Roger Bruns

FRANKLIN D. ROOSEVELT

A Biography

Jeffrey W. Coker

GREENWOOD BIOGRAPHIES

GREENWOOD PRESS
WESTPORT, CONNECTICUT · LONDON

Library of Congress Cataloging-in-Publication Data

Coker, Jeffrey W.
    Franklin D. Roosevelt : a biography / Jeffrey W. Coker.
        p. cm.—(Greenwood biographies, ISSN 1540-4900)
    Includes bibliographical references and index.
    ISBN: 0-313–32337–2 (alk. paper)
    1. Roosevelt, Franklin D. (Franklin Delano), 1882–1945. 2. Presidents—United
States—Biography. I. Title. II. Series.
E807.C56   2005
937.917′092—dc22   2005010762

British Library Cataloguing in Publication Data is available.

Library of Congress Catalog Card Number: 200501762
ISBN: 0–313–32337–2
ISSN: 1540–4900

First published in 2005

Greenwood Press, 88 Post Road West, Westport, CT 06881
An imprint of Greenwood Publishing Group, Inc.
www.greenwood.com

Printed in the United States of America

The paper used in this book complies with the
Permanent Paper Standard issued by the National
Information Standards Organization (Z39.48–1984).

10 9 8 7 6 5 4 3 2 1

CONTENTS

SERIES FOREWORD

In response to high school and public library needs, Greenwood developed this distinguished series of full-length biographies specifically for student use. Prepared by field experts and professionals, these engaging biographies are tailored for high school students who need challenging yet accessible biographies. Ideal for secondary school assignments, the length, format and subject areas are designed to meet educators' requirements and students' interests.

Greenwood offers an extensive selection of biographies spanning all curriculum related subject areas including social studies, the sciences, literature and the arts, history and politics, as well as popular culture, covering public figures and famous personalities from all time periods and backgrounds, both historic and contemporary, who have made an impact on American and/or world culture. Greenwood biographies were chosen based on comprehensive feedback from librarians and educators. Consideration was given to both curriculum relevance and inherent interest. The result is an intriguing mix of the well known and the unexpected, the saints and sinners from long-ago history and contemporary pop culture. Readers will find a wide array of subject choices from fascinating crime figures like Al Capone to inspiring pioneers like Margaret Mead, from the greatest minds of our time like Stephen Hawking to the most amazing success stories of our day like J. K. Rowling.

While the emphasis is on fact, not glorification, the books are meant to be fun to read. Each volume provides in-depth information about the subject's life from birth through childhood, the teen years, and adulthood.

A thorough account relates family background and education, traces personal and professional influences, and explores struggles, accomplishments, and contributions. A timeline highlights the most significant life events against a historical perspective. Bibliographies supplement the reference value of each volume.

PREFACE

In what has become an annual tradition, pollsters ask historians to rank the presidents in order of greatness. The intent of these exercises is to draw upon expert opinion to learn more about presidential leadership, but for the most part they confirm the views of the broader public. The usual names appear at the top of these lists, year in and year out: George Washington, Thomas Jefferson, Abraham Lincoln, and Theodore Roosevelt, to name a few.

Franklin Delano Roosevelt is another name that appears consistently at the top of such lists as America's greatest president. He was, after all, the president who carried the nation through the Great Depression as "Dr. New Deal" and also guided it during World War II as "Dr. Win-the-War." He won election an unprecedented four times and, according to many historians, brought about a reordering of the country's political landscape. His popularity, then and now, encourages a great deal of mythologizing. Oftentimes, the actual Roosevelt is crowded out by the image of Roosevelt.

Who was this man who served as commander-in-chief for an unprecedented 13 years? Was he the ever-optimistic, "can-do" Roosevelt, smiling as a long cigarette-holder protruded from the corner of his lips? Was he the cunning, perhaps even devious, politician who possessed an uncanny ability to manipulate those around him? Was he the great orator who was able to shroud indecision with an ability to appeal to a public audience? Was he a true reformer who sought to uplift the powerless? Was he instead the aristocrat-turned-politico who capitalized on prevailing political winds to vault into power? All of these images and more have appeared as "versions" of Roosevelt.

The life of Franklin Roosevelt offers a study into the question of leadership. Few who encountered him, even his opponents, would deny that he was an effective leader. A great number of experts in the areas of politics, sociology, and history have sought to explain the sources of political charisma. What makes a great leader? In the case of Roosevelt, the question is not easily answered. He was not the greatest public speaker of his age; many opponents whom Roosevelt defeated were more gifted speakers. He was not unattractive, but few would argue that his political career was due to good looks. He had a solid education but was by no means an intellectual figure. Yet there was something in the Roosevelt persona that appealed to millions of Americans, during his lifetime and after.

The story of Franklin Roosevelt is also the story of the United States in the first half of the twentieth century. Roosevelt was born at the height of the industrial age, came of age just as the country was becoming a world power, and first entered public service just as the world was plunging into war. His rise in politics as a progressive reformer was a sign that Americans were altering their perceptions of the government's role in their lives. His presidency took place during the most severe and prolonged economic crisis in the country's history, followed by a global war that transformed the role of the United States in world affairs. The changes that occurred during his lifetime were dramatic and far-reaching.

This book offers an introduction to the life of FDR and his America. Readers will encounter the major events and turning points of his life: his early years at home in Hyde Park, New York, his education at Groton and Harvard, his entrance into political life, and his rise to national prominence. For each part of his life, there is, of course, a much more detailed story to tell. Hopefully, readers will be inspired to investigate further into the extraordinary life of Roosevelt and the vast amount of historical writing about him.

Most of the quotations offered herein are culled from published collections of Roosevelt's public speeches and private correspondences, particularly Elliott Roosevelt, ed., *FDR: His Personal Letters* (New York: Duell, Sloan, and Pearce, 1947–50) and Samuel Rosenman, ed., *The Public Papers and Addresses of Franklin D. Roosevelt*, 13 vols. (New York: Random House, 1938–50). An enormous amount of secondary literature exists on Roosevelt. Readers are encouraged to consult the bibliographic essay for some of the sources consulted for the writing of this book.

ACKNOWLEDGMENTS

The author would like to express gratitude to Kevin Ohe and Michael Hermann at Greenwood Press for making this book possible. Kevin first contacted me about the project; Michael exhibited admirable patience in seeing it through to completion. My colleagues at Belmont University have my deepest respect and admiration—thanks to Brenda Jackson, Doug Bisson, Cindy Bisson, Dan Schafer, Larry Hall, Larry German, Thom Storey, and others for their friendship and camaraderie over the years. David Smith, longtime friend and fellow Texan, has been there through thick and thin. My father, Tim Coker, has done more for me than I could ever express in words. Finally, my wife and best friend, Jennifer Reed Coker, deserves far more than I will ever be able to return. The best I can do here is to say thank you, now and always.

TIMELINE

30 January 1882	Franklin D. Roosevelt born in Hyde Park, New York
September 1896	Enters Groton preparatory school
September 1899	Enrolls at Harvard University
December 1900	James Roosevelt, FDR's father, dies
September 1904	Enrolls at Columbia University Law School (for one year)
March 1905	Marries Anna Eleanor Roosevelt
May 1906	Daughter Anna Eleanor Roosevelt born
September 1907	Begins clerkship with law firm of Carter, Ledyard, and Milburn, New York City
December 1907	Son James Roosevelt born
March 1909	Son Franklin Delano Roosevelt, Jr. born (dies in November)
September 1910	Son Elliott born
November 1910	Wins election to New York Senate
November 1912	Wins reelection to New York Senate
January 1913	Begins tenure as assistant secretary of the Navy
August 1914	World War I begins
August 1914	Son Franklin Delano Roosevelt, Jr. born
March 1916	Son John Aspinwall Roosevelt born
April 1917	United States enters World War I

November 1918	World War I ends
June 1920	Wins nomination for vice president; loses election in November
August 1921	Diagnosed with poliomyelitis
June 1924	Returns to politics by attending Democratic National Convention
February 1927	Acquires Warm Springs resort property in Georgia
November 1928	Elected governor of New York
October 1929	Stock market crashes; beginning of Great Depression
November 1930	Wins reelection bid for governor of New York
November 1932	Wins presidential election over Republican incumbent Herbert Hoover
February 1933	Survives assassination attempt in Miami, Florida
March 1933	Delivers first "fireside chat"
March 1933	Beginning of the Hundred Days
May 1935	Supreme Court rules against National Industrial Recovery Act
January 1936	Supreme Court rules against Agricultural Adjustment Act
November 1936	Wins reelection over Republican Alf Landon
February 1937	Court packing scheme begins
October 1937	Delivers "quarantine speech"
Spring 1938	FDR's attempt to "purge" Democratic party begins
August 1939	Nazi-Soviet Pact announced
September 1939	Germany invades Poland; World War II begins
November 1939	United States begins "cash and carry" trade with countries at war
September 1940	FDR signs Selective Service Act
September 1940	"Destroyers-for-bases" trading begins
November 1940	Wins election to third term over Republican Wendell L. Willkie
March 1941	"Lend-lease" trade with Great Britain begins
June 1941	Germany invades the Soviet Union

August 1941	Atlantic Charter issued by FDR and Winston Churchill
September 1941	Mother, Sara Delano Roosevelt, dies
December 1941	Japanese attack on Pearl Harbor
February 1942	Internment of Japanese Americans begins (Executive Order 9066)
February 1942	Allied invasion of North Africa begins
January 1943	FDR and Churchill meet at Casablanca, announce "unconditional surrender" policy
July 1943	Allied invasion of Italy begins
November 1943	FDR meets with Churchill and Stalin at Tehran, Iran
June 1944	Invasion of Normandy (D-Day) begins
November 1944	Wins election to fourth term over Republican Thomas Dewey
February 1945	Meets with Churchill and Stalin at Yalta
12 April 1945	Dies at Warm Springs, Georgia; buried at Hyde Park, New York, on April 15

Chapter 1

BEGINNINGS

"Never, oh never!" Sara Delano Roosevelt remarked to a reporter about her son just after he had won the 1932 presidential election. "That was the last thing I should ever imagined for him." Few who knew Franklin Roosevelt in his youth would have predicted a career in politics.

Roosevelt's childhood was anything but typical for nineteenth-century America. The family lived in what one historian has called the "most aristocratic community ever established in America." The Hudson River Valley, and particularly the area in and around Hyde Park, New York, was the historic home for a number of the country's leading families—some of whom traced their arrival to the seventeenth century. There was something "old worldish" about the region. Modest Dutch farmers, who settled the region in the 1600s, with time had carved out massive landholdings that over the centuries became hereditary estates. The region retained much of the class system of Europe. The landed gentry, or "patroons," erected a semi-feudal world based upon agriculture and tenant labor. By the time of the Civil War, some of these families, such as the Livingstons and the Van Rensselaers, had lived as aristocrats for more than two hundred years.

Yet the rhythms of this Old World aristocracy began to change after the Civil War, as entrepreneurs from the cities, having made large fortunes during a wave of industrial expansion, began to arrive and seek entry into the ranks of American royalty. These "new money" families were of a different sort. They seldom were of Dutch ancestry, had little respect for lineage and "breeding," and tended to be more garish in a desire to flaunt their newfound wealth. While the Dutch elite of the region lived in modest manors (albeit large and splendorous homes compared to most), the new arrivals built enormous, gaudy mansions seemingly with a goal of making up for their lack of pedigree. Vanderbilts, Carnegies, and Rockefellers—the families of those "titans of industry" who transformed the United States in the late nineteenth century and made incredible fortunes in the process—soon began to dominate the social scene. For the older families, these new arrivals were seen as crude and overbearing.

The Roosevelts definitely were a part of the "old money" class. The first arrival in New York was a farmer named Nicholas Claes Martenzen von Rosenvelt, who came from Holland in the early 1600s and established a small farm on the island of Manhattan. Over the next century, the descendents of von Rosenvelt Americanized the family name, dropping "von" and ultimately developing it into the name Roosevelt. The family also became more prosperous, all the while moving northward to escape the increasing population of New York City. As early as 1700, the first Roosevelts began to arrive in the Hudson River Valley, which over the next 150 years would become home for several branches of the family.

There had been a time, of course, when the Roosevelts themselves were "new money." Among the more successful of the earlier Roosevelts was Franklin's great-great grandfather Isaac, who invested his modest inheritance in a Manhattan sugar refinery. By the time of the Revolutionary War, Isaac Roosevelt had become a leader in New York society. He married the daughter of a wealthy scion of the city and was active in local politics. Like most businessmen involved in export commodities, Isaac certainly would have chafed at the restrictive trade policies the British enacted in the 1760s, which included attempts to control and tax the sugar trade. After offering financial support for the Revolution, he helped to found the Bank of New York in 1784. At the height of his career, in 1788, Isaac Roosevelt served as a member of the New York state convention that ratified the United States Constitution. By the time of his death in 1794, the family business, now called Roosevelt and Son's, along with other investments and ventures, had established a family fortune. Descendents of Isaac, including Franklin, would live a life of leisure and opportunity.

Franklin's father James, grandson of Isaac, was born in 1828 and indeed lived a life of ease. Yet James Roosevelt was not lazy; he spent a lifetime attempting to build upon the impressive achievements of the family. Although he never made a fortune, his ventures were successful enough to maintain the family's high status. He tried just about everything. After graduating from Union College and Harvard Law School, he attempted a career in law but soon grew restless and plunged into a series of entrepreneurial ventures. There was a venture in coal, as he became director of Consolidated Coal Company with the aid of an uncle. He became involved in the booming railroad industry and was named president of the Southern Railway Security Company, which invested heavily in railroad development in the South after the Civil War. In the 1880s, James joined with a group of investors to form the Maritime Canal Company, which promoted the construction of a canal in Nicaragua connecting the Atlantic Ocean with the Pacific. The venture proved ill-fated, despite James spending time in Washington lobbying for governmental support for the idea.

Students of the Roosevelt family conclude that James Roosevelt was an able, but not impressive, businessman. Perhaps the reason he never amassed the great fortune he sought was due, at least in part, to his comfortable background. If Roosevelt enjoyed the opportunities of a fine education and plenty of venture capital, he perhaps lacked the ambition of an Andrew Carnegie or John D. Rockefeller, whose climbs to economic power came from an intense desire to rise up from humble origins. James was a gentleman first, a businessman second. In fact, displays of excessive drive and ambition were considered unseemly for the gentry of New York.

James Roosevelt, as a gentleman of means, was expected to select a wife fitting of his station, which he did at the age of 25. Rebecca Howland was the daughter of another wealthy Hudson River family, and in 1854 the couple had their first child, son James Roosevelt, nicknamed Rosey. The three lived a happy life together for years. Locals referred to him as "Mr. James," and a bucolic setting of well-manicured lawns and dairy cows offered the family a peaceful and stable life. This harmony ended abruptly when Rebecca died in 1876. Son James was almost grown by this time—he graduated from Columbia the following year and would soon marry Helen Astor—which meant that, despite his age, "Mr. James" was among the more eligible bachelors in the area.

Bachelorhood did not last long for him. In 1880, he met Sara Delano, the daughter of another well-to-do family in Hyde Park. Her father, Warren Delano, was a successful businessman who, despite stretches of financial difficulty, managed to amass a considerable fortune, including significant wealth from trade in East Asia, including the trafficking of opium. Sara, born in 1854, grew up on the family estate of Algonac, a stately, lavish mansion close to Springwood. Only 26 when she met James, Sara had developed into a charming, graceful young woman. She also had a keen mind and an exceptional education, having traveled with her parents around the world. During her childhood she had lived in Hong Kong, France, and Germany. Now she would marry James Roosevelt, a man twice her age—an arrangement that evidently pleased both families.

Sara became pregnant with her first and only son in 1882, during the couple's 10-month honeymoon tour of Europe. James's second son, according to tradition, should have been named Isaac, but here Sara's strong influence on her son began. She evidently abhorred the name and insisted on Franklin, in honor of her uncle, with her maiden name to serve as his middle appellation. Considering the very close relationship she would have with her son, the decision was appropriate (she even was known to say with pride that Franklin was a Delano, not a Roosevelt). While Franklin and his father always maintained a cordial relationship, his mother constantly was at his side and remained a close companion for most of his life.

Franklin's childhood was sheltered, stable, and happy. He was, in essence, an only child, surrounded by a doting mother, the staff at Springwood, and relatives who lived nearby. Despite the close relationship between Franklin and Sara, the young boy was encouraged to pursue masculine interests. He later recalled an active interest in woodworking, gymnastics, and hunting. His greatest love, however, was sailing. Beginning in 1882, the family vacationed regularly at the island of Campobello, off the coast of Maine in the Bay of Fundy. Each year, Franklin was able to hone his skills as a seaman. His father purchased a sailing yacht, the *Half-Moon*, which allowed Franklin to learn to handle himself on the seas. When he turned 16, he received his own 21-foot vessel, dubbed the *New Moon*. These experiences gave Franklin a fondness for maritime activities that would remain with him for the rest of his life.

As was typical of children of the well-to-do, Franklin did not attend school away from home but received instruction from a series of governesses. His favorite was a Swiss teacher named Jeanne Sandoz, with whom he studied from 1891 to 1893. His education was wide-ranging and included history, mathematics, and foreign languages. Mlle. Sandoz particularly stressed French, and after a few years Franklin became fluent in the language. His education was quite liberal in the sense that he often was allowed to select readings and lessons based on his own interests. By all accounts he was an inquisitive boy, a trait very much encouraged by his parents. Among the many hobbies he counted were bird collecting and stamp collecting. He became somewhat of an expert in identifying bird species of the area and would display his knowledge to anyone willing to listen. The Roosevelts raised a confident, if somewhat self-centered, boy of considerable talent and promise.

The young Franklin also was accustomed to being the center of attention, and the sheltered nature of his youth must have been apparent to his parents. Most of his peers who had been taught within the home ventured out into a school setting at the age of 12. Franklin, too, was ready to enroll in school at that age, yet his parents, perhaps concerned that he was not quite ready to leave home, held him back from school until the age of 14.

Although there were several schooling options for the sons of Hudson Valley scions, James and Sara had for some time agreed that the best place for Franklin was Groton, a relatively new school in Connecticut near the Nashua River. A great deal of writing exists on the influence of Groton in forming Roosevelt's worldview. Historians often seek out pivotal experiences in the lives of individuals, and more than one has concluded that Franklin's years at Groton may have been most responsible for the formation of his character. Roosevelt often spoke of Groton's impact, particularly the school's founder and rector, Endicott Peabody.

In many respects, Groton was the embodiment of Rector Peabody, who founded the school in 1882 by soliciting financial support from the elite of New England society. Counted among its board of trustees in the early years was the financial mogul J. P. Morgan, along with leading clergymen Phillips Brooks and William Lawrence. Peabody's own family was part of high society. His father, a wealthy investor and partner of Morgan, sent him to England for an education that culminated in a degree from Cambridge University. While at Cambridge, he came under the influence of Charles Kingsley, a professor who championed Christian-rooted social reform. While the Peabody family was not devoutly religious, young Endicott made Christian values the center of his life and his school.

Peabody developed aspirations of creating a school in the United States along the lines of Rugby, a British preparatory school founded by reformer Thomas Arnold. Rugby had taken as its mission the goal of inculcating England's next generation of leaders with a Christian education, with a strong element of moralism and duty to fellow men. Peabody returned to the United States to do the same. Yet while Rugby had been built upon a heritage of aristocracy in the Old World, Peabody's Groton faced the challenge of being a school for the elite in a society that spurned sharp class divisions. At a time when most education reformers stressed democracy and equal access to schools, Peabody attempted to build a school where the "best families" of New England would send their sons to prepare them for future positions of leadership.

By 1896, when Franklin first arrived at Groton, the new school already had a reputation as being perhaps the most elite school in the entire region. Years later, in fact, Josephus Daniels, under whom Roosevelt served during World War I, remarked that, of all of Roosevelt's potential liabilities as a candidate for public office, the fact that he attended Groton perhaps would be the most difficult to overcome, as it emphasized his aristocratic upbringing. The school's physical appearance lived up to its image. The campus lay just outside the sleepy village of Groton, along the Nashua River, with a breathtaking view from the hilltop on which its buildings sat majestically. The architecture also added to the atmosphere—the campus featured a wooden, Georgian-style chapel flanked by brick buildings that housed classrooms, offices, and dormitories. Impressive elm trees punctuated impeccably kept greens, with athletic fields forming the backdrop. In this idyllic, secluded setting, Groton sought to develop the leaders of the next generation.

Although the adjustment from being an only child to living in a boarding school was difficult, Franklin gradually found his stride and ultimately flourished at Groton. The school was steadfastly regimented; surprisingly, Roosevelt took a liking to the strict rules and regulations. While letters home might have complained about cramped living quarters, cold showers, and a general lack of amenities that he was accustomed to at Springwood, instead they were full of cheer, indicating that Franklin met all challenges with a spirit of conquest. He genuinely enjoyed the culture of the school and strove to make his mark socially and academically.

Groton did present significant social challenges. Because his parents decided to wait until Franklin was 14 before allowing him to enroll, he came in two years later than almost all of his classmates. The first year at Groton, called Form I, was a time when the boys developed strong ties of friendship. Franklin entered Form III as an outsider, and it would take some time and effort to fit in. There were other challenges. One was the erratic personality of his cousin Taddy, already enrolled, who had trouble fitting in. Rosy, as the other boys called him, was an odd boy who seemed to enjoy being an outcast and also spent much time being disciplined by Peabody. The Roosevelt name, then, was already besmirched when Franklin arrived, and the boys branded him with the nickname "Uncle Frank," forming an unfortunate link between him and his problematic cousin.

Another problem was Franklin's demeanor, which often came off as somewhat affected and snobbish. Much of this had to do with the fact that Franklin had grown up at rather secluded Springwood surrounded by adults. He also had spent a great deal of time abroad and in the presence of foreign-born instructors, experiences that allowed him to learn French and German well but left a peculiar mark on his New England dialect.

He did not sound like the other boys; on more than one occasion, fellow students remembered his speech as sounding European. A boy facing such social impediments might have overcome them with a strong and extroverted personality. Unfortunately, and again linked to his early life experiences, Franklin was rather shy. For a boy raised as the center of attention in an adult-oriented household, the conformist nature of Groton would prove something of a shock.

Gradually, though, Franklin learned to fit in at the school and embrace its conformity. While athletic prowess would have yielded social dividends at a place where football was an obsession (many of Franklin's letters home opened with comments on the triumphs and travails of the Groton's starting "eleven"), he was not so gifted. But he never gave up, on athletics or on any other opportunity, becoming an enthusiastic joiner of just about every club or activity that came his way. Whether it was the appointment, during his final year, as a dormitory prefect, or his casting for a role in a school play, Roosevelt plunged into activities as if each was the most important experience of his life. Yet interestingly, this enthusiasm, which shone forth in letter after letter to his parents, must have been guarded in public. Students and faculty remembered Franklin not for his enthusiasm and energy, but rather as calm, reflective, and detached. Peabody described him in his final grading report simply as a "faithful scholar"; more revealingly, many years later Peabody wrote these oft-repeated words about his recollections of Roosevelt: "He was a quiet, satisfactory boy of more than ordinary intelligence, taking a good position in his Form but not brilliant. Athletically he was rather too slight for success. We all liked him."

Roosevelt matriculated to Harvard University a young man with a complex personality. A serious student, he was average intellectually. He worked very hard to be popular but was often considered aloof. He did possess self-confidence, however, which was aided by a relatively smooth transition into college due to the fact that many of his fellow Grotonians arrived with him. Lathrop Brown, a friend dating back to his boyhood, was his roommate. If his entry to Groton had been somewhat rocky, his arrival at Harvard found him surrounded by an established social network. Roosevelt moved into a very nice private dormitory in an area near campus called the "Gold Coast" because of its affluent residents. Compared to the modest on-campus dormitories, Franklin's abode would have seemed palatial—he had his own bedroom, a large sitting room, and a private bath.

The Gold Coast residence was but one marker of a class divide that existed at turn-of-the-century Harvard. A number of students came from far-away places referred to passively as the "provinces" and enrolled based on their academic merit. Studious, serious, and highly ambitious, these students tended to be quite respectful of their professors, at times perhaps even awestruck by their academic prowess. One professor at the time re-marked that such students tended to "hover in the background," working diligently, attending sporting events, but leaving little mark on the social environment on campus.

Roosevelt's circle was quite different; Gold Coast residents were part of an elite class of students who arrived at Harvard based more on their social standing in New England or New York than achievement. These students were outspoken, sometimes brash, and approached attendance at Harvard as an expected rite of passage rather than a life-determining opportunity. By most accounts, there was a unique code of conduct among them. One should not be too ambitious, too intellectual, nor too eager. Professors were to be tolerated rather than idolized. Most importantly, college life revolved around an active social life based on membership in a complex network of clubs and fraternal organizations. In fact, one's inclusion in these groups was critical in determining not only one's success at Harvard, but most likely in life after college. As a member of the elite students, Roosevelt automatically was a candidate for the most exclusive clubs. Let-ters sent home during his first year indicate that foremost on Franklin's mind was his admission into the "Institute of 1770," Delta Kappa Epsilon (or "Dickeys"), and the most prestigious of all, Porcellian. These clubs were reserved for the social elite of New England—families on the social registry who had attended the appropriate preparatory schools and would eventually take their places at the heads of U.S. business and law.

Roosevelt's social life at Harvard always took precedence over his stud-ies. He lobbied very hard to be included in the most prestigious clubs and was quite hurt when he was excluded from Porcellian. He did, however, achieve membership in most others. He also was an avid follower of sports and wanted very much to participate, as he had at Groton. He went out for the football team but was cut due to a lack of athleticism. Letters sent home during these years always mentioned social activities and sporting events. Very seldom did he comment on academic matters.

His lack of interest in intellectual pursuit was reflected in his grades. Never a poor student, Franklin never excelled in the classroom either. Harvard in these years was becoming an academic powerhouse under the leadership of President Charles W. Eliot, who sought to catapult Harvard from a genteel institution for New England's wealthiest children into a research-oriented university. Roosevelt had the opportunity to take courses from some of the leading intellectuals in the United States at the time, including a history course from the renowned Frederick Jackson Turner and philosophy courses from looming figures such as Josiah Royce and William James. Yet these experiences hardly were transforming for him. He usually made grades of B or C in his classes and seldom made much of an impression on his professors. For the most part, he found academic pursuits boring.

Perhaps the most rewarding activity of Roosevelt's years at college was his work on the campus newspaper, *The Harvard Crimson*. In his capacity as reporter, and as editor during his senior year, he found an avenue for the social interaction that he found so appealing. Although he worked energetically and enthusiastically on the newspaper, his journalism was not hard-hitting. Most of his articles focused on mundane matters such as calling for school spirit or support for athletic teams. However, Franklin sincerely loved the work, and his memories of serving on the newspaper staff were among his fondest.

Graduating from Harvard was one of two pivotal events in the life of the young Roosevelt. The other was marrying Eleanor Roosevelt. A niece of Theodore Roosevelt and daughter of Franklin's godparents, she had met Franklin a few times during their childhood years. However, when Franklin spent time with her at a family gathering in 1903, he was swept off his feet. She was, in many ways, his perfect match. Obviously, she came from an acceptable family and had the proper background and social standing that would be expected. Her education had been exceptional, and she displayed a remarkable refinement and maturity. For the energetic, even rambunctious, Franklin, Eleanor's primary attraction may have been her seriousness and calm.

Despite her outward demeanor, Eleanor lacked confidence as a young woman, perhaps due to a troubled childhood. Although she was financially secure, her family had been besieged with upheaval. Her father was a handsome and gregarious man who drank heavily and spent much of his time away from home, usually in attempts to improve his often-poor health. Eleanor idolized him. Meanwhile, her mother struck a startling contrast. She was devoutly religious, quite strict, and very critical. Eleanor was awkward as a girl, somewhat lanky and gangly, and her mother often made disparaging comments about her appearance and called her "Granny." Both of her parents died when she was a little girl; Eleanor was then raised by her grandmother.

As time passed and Eleanor moved into adolescence, she began to grow into a graceful young woman. Never a natural beauty, she did strike a noble pose—several observers referred to her as "handsome." Her education had been top-notch, carried out by private tutors and including several extended trips abroad. By the time she met her distant cousin Franklin at the beginning of their courtship, she seemingly had overcome her troubled youth. But while Franklin was enraptured, his mother was very much against the marriage, and this proved to be a difficult hurdle. Yet due to Franklin's lobbying, and no doubt due to the fact that Eleanor was in fact an excellent choice for her son, Sara finally relented. They were married in New York on March 17, 1905.

The young couple soon settled in to family life. Eleanor gave birth to their first child during their first year together and over the next 12 years had four more. Of obvious concern at this time was Franklin's professional future. In the autumn of 1904, he entered law school at Columbia University while the family settled in to a nice home in Manhattan. As had been the case at Harvard, Franklin was an adequate student, but certainly not stellar. The main problem was his lack of interest in the details of legal study. After a year of average grades, he dropped out. However, he did pick up enough education to pass the New York State bar examination and soon found a position with Carter, Ledyard, and Milburn, a successful corporate firm in the city.

Life as an attorney was not exactly fulfilling. Although his work did allow him to enter into important professional and social circles in New York, there was something about the job that lacked substance. He worked on a few important cases, but as a young member of the firm he spent most of his time dealing with small claims against various clients. He often spent his days working at the court house, surrounded by people very different from the high society types with whom he usually associated. Roosevelt enjoyed the atmosphere and was surprised by his ability to connect with those who were not part of New York's social registry. Still, it became increasingly clear that Franklin wanted something more out of life than a comfortable legal career.

The outlet he was looking for was politics. When Roosevelt decided to pursue a life in public service is not altogether clear. He had shown an interest in affairs of state, particularly foreign policy, in college. Even at Groton, history classes, particularly political history, tended to be his favorites. However, a strong check on this interest was his social position. For most people in Roosevelt's genteel world, politics was considered something not worthy of a dignified gentleman. This clearly was the attitude of Franklin's mother, who from the beginning had little enthusiasm for the idea that her son might become a politician.

At the same time, there were, of course, strong political figures in the family. Franklin's father, while not a career politician, always had been quite active in the local political scene in Hyde Park. Yet the most influential figure of all was his cousin Theodore Roosevelt, who had ascended to the presidency during Franklin's freshman year at Harvard. On several occasions Franklin visited the White House and discussed issues with Teddy. If one story is to be believed, by the time he had entered law school, Franklin already had charted his political future, explaining to a fellow student that his path to the presidency would mirror that of his famous cousin—first a cabinet-level position, followed by the governorship of New York, and ultimately the White House. Whether the story is true or not, once Franklin made the decision to enter political life, he clearly had lofty ambitions.

Desiring to enter politics is one thing; actually finding an opportunity to do so is another. However, once Franklin did decide on this course of action, his emergence into New York political life was rapid. While working at the law firm, he began to make inquiries into the possibility of running for a seat in the New York state legislature. He soon discovered that there might be an opportunity to run for the Senate. With help from attorney John E. Mack, an influential Democrat from Roosevelt's home county, he won the nomination and soon found himself in his first campaign.

The decision to run as a Democrat was in many ways a foregone conclusion, but it also could have been political suicide in the Republican-dominated state of New York. Cousin Theodore may have been an important inspiration, but his father's legacy in some ways proved more lasting. While many Roosevelts were Republicans, Franklin's branch of the family tree historically were Democrats, and evidently Franklin never considered the alternative. All indications pointed to Roosevelt being better off by switching party affiliations. New York was a Republican state, his home district overwhelmingly had voted Republican in recent years, and he would be able to count Teddy as a powerful ally. Yet, despite all of this, the question evidently never was open to question.

In the political arena, timing often is the most important element in determining success. The 1910 election was the first of many instances where Franklin Roosevelt displayed an extraordinary sense of timing. Running as a Democrat in years past had been an enormous liability, but the ground had quietly been shifting. Across the nation, the Republican party had been experiencing a serious rift between a "progressive" wing and more traditional elements. Theodore Roosevelt gradually became the standard-bearer of the progressive side of the party. In many states, including New York, these so-called insurgents had begun to challenge the entrenched party leadership. Infighting among Republicans began to open doors for Democratic party challengers—in many areas for the first time in decades.

Franklin intuitively sensed the pulse of progressive ideas in New York, and his campaign hoped to attract reform-minded voters in both parties. The message that resonated most with the people was a call for "clean government"—a challenge to the machine politics that controlled New York City and the capital in Albany. For decades, the Democratic party had been dominated by a close-knit circle of operatives known as the Tammany ring. Working through patronage, and often through corruption, Tammany leaders controlled who won nominations in the party, who received financial support in elections, and then often controlled their votes once in office. For a Democrat, running for office without the blessing of Tammany leaders was a recipe for defeat.

Yet Roosevelt not only ran without direct support from Tammany leaders, he ran on a platform that directly attacked them. During the campaign, he railed against the "bossism" that dominated his party, particularly the leadership of Charles F. Murphy, who headed Tammany. While such rhetoric might have been foolhardy in New York City, there actually was a growing frustration with machine politics in the rural portions of the state. What in the past would have been considered an assurance of defeat became something of an asset for Roosevelt. In fact, his message of reforming government even won over many Republican voters.

Although his first campaign speeches were awkward, he soon developed a comfortable style that seemed to work well with voters. While campaigning was considered a grind for many politicians, Roosevelt actually enjoyed it. He ran an intense campaign, covering every inch of ground in his district by touring in a bright red automobile. The move was a gamble, given that in some rural areas people had not even seen a motor car. Yet everywhere he traveled, crowds turned out to hear him, and most came away with a positive attitude about the new candidate. Finally, the Roosevelt name did emerge as a factor in the election. While Teddy would have preferred that his youthful relative follow in his footsteps as a Republican, family ties went deeper than party lines. The popular president, now out of office for over a year, could have influenced the election by campaigning for the Republican candidate. However, Theodore Roosevelt had little interest in saving this rural district for the Republicans. He refused to travel there during the campaign or speak directly on the election.

Teddy's decision to abstain from the election gave Franklin the opportunity to capitalize on the Roosevelt name, for while he did not get public support from his larger-than-life cousin, he seldom was challenged on the matter of party affiliation. All of these factors led to impressive victory for Franklin Roosevelt, who came into office as part of a wave of Democrats who entered government in New York and across the country. The political tide was turning in the United States. Roosevelt, a Democrat with a powerful political name, was now well-positioned to ride it to even greater heights.

Chapter 2

LEARNING THE ROPES

Roosevelt's entry into politics began during a turning point in U.S. political life. The Progressive Era, which began around 1900, brought about a reordering of the political landscape in almost every state and played a significant role in national politics as well. Progressivism meant different things to different people, but at its core was an attempt to come to terms with the late nineteenth century, particularly the rapid pace of change brought about by industrialization, urbanization, and immigration. Progressive reformers also challenged government corruption, advocated for the expansion of the franchise, and sponsored a range of new laws designed to regulate labor practices, education, and other social welfare issues.

Reformers who rallied to the Progressive cause did not fall into a single political party, nor did they all operate at the same level of government. Within both major parties, elements sprang up after 1900 that championed reform. Despite the efforts of some, even Theodore Roosevelt himself, to pull progressives together into a new political organization, the traditional two-party system held firm. However, the emergence of progressive reformers was a challenge to both parties, each of which had to figure out ways to bridge the gap between these elements and more traditional-minded party members. As the Progressive movement gathered steam, each party adopted positions advanced by reformers, and, with time, individual progressives moved into positions of leadership. By the time the United States entered World War I, the label "progressive" could be an asset for members of either party.

Franklin Roosevelt, then, was the beneficiary of good timing on a number of fronts. As a young Democrat, he entered political life during a time of resurgence for the party, and for the next several years was able to capitalize on the growing strength of the party nationally. Because he had run his first campaign as a progressive reformer, he also benefited from the increasing support for reform in both parties. In many respects, whether he knew it or not, as he took his seat in the New York State Senate, Roosevelt was well positioned for a rise to prominence.

Franklin and Eleanor, now with four young children, moved into an apartment in Albany in January 1911, just before the beginning of the upcoming congressional session. From the beginning, Roosevelt established himself as a force with which to be reckoned, particularly with respect to those Tammany Hall leaders in New York City who had been the recipients of so much criticism by Roosevelt during his campaign. His first showdown, and one that would establish him as a leader of the progressive voice in the New York assembly, centered on the election of the next United States Senator for New York. Because this occurred before the ratification of the 17th Amendment to the United States Constitution, providing for the direct election of senators, New York still elected its representatives for the upper house of Congress in the state legislature.

This particular confrontation began when United States Senator Chauncy M. Depew decided to retire. Because the Democrats had just taken control of the New York legislature, for the first time in years they would be in a position to determine his predecessor—provided that they could maintain unity. From the beginning, Roosevelt and a small group of like-minded colleagues squared off against Tammany Hall and the New York City–based elements of the party. Charles F. Murphy already had been working behind the scenes to win the nomination for business tycoon and longtime politician William F. Sheehan. Roosevelt, who had begun to make the rounds in and around the assembly house, had concluded that there were several more qualified candidates; he ultimately settled on Edward M. Sheppard, an attorney from Brooklyn with no ties to the Tammany ring. With the backing of Murphy and his associates in the senate, it would be an uphill battle for Roosevelt and the other, so-called insurgents.

What was most notable about the entire affair was Roosevelt's willingness, at the young age of 30, to rise as a vocal leader of the insurgents. This was his first political experience, and his actions here would play a large role in defining his career as a state senator. Taking on Tammany and the entrenched party leadership was a large gamble. If things turned out badly for Roosevelt, he potentially could lose all allies in the party and render his position in the legislature powerless. Furthermore, the insurgents were a minority—the larger portion of Democrats were willing to follow the line of the leadership. Unclear to Roosevelt and the other insurgents was whether they had large enough numbers to matter. Even if they did, any defections could mean defeat. In many ways, the deck clearly was stacked against Roosevelt in the battle.

The insurgents, however, did have some hope. Many people viewed the matter in light of larger concerns over electoral reform. Progressives claimed that senate elections should be decided by voters rather than leg-islators. Roosevelt could use this sentiment to paint Murphy and Tam-many as a textbook example of the way that political leaders could be chosen in smoke-filled legislative chambers. The issue was one Roosevelt believed in sincerely, and his conviction gave him strength and energy.

He would need both. When the Democratic leadership realized that the insurgents had enough supporters to block the election of any par-ticular candidate, both sides settled in for a protracted battle. At times the situation became rather heated. Supporters for Sheehan, who was of Irish ancestry, charged that Roosevelt and others on his side opposed him due to his ethnicity and his religion. The accusation that Roosevelt was guilty of what would have been called "Knownothingism" in an earlier time—opposition to immigrants, particularly Irish Catholics—could be stinging to Roosevelt, a patrician of Dutch ancestry. Insurgents responded by claiming that their position had nothing to do with the identity of the candidate but only his qualifications.

Both sides dug in for a heated battle, and the controversy carried on through February and March. Week after week, each side worked to nego-tiate with the other, all the while blasting their opponents publicly. Each side also had to consider the Republican members of the senate, for while they were not the majority, their actions could be decisive given divisions among Democrats. By the end of March, however, Roosevelt began to see the battle was lost. Individual insurgents were beginning to weaken, and the party leadership sought out compromise candidates. In the end they advanced James A. O'Gorman, a judge with a strong record but who also was a loyal Tammany man. Roosevelt resisted his candidacy at the outset, but as more insurgents began to make it clear that it was time to move on, he too relented.

This battle against the entrenched leadership of the party, while a de-feat for Roosevelt, may have been a boost to his career for two reasons. First, the campaign against Tammany gave the insurgents good press cov-erage, as many newspaper reporters statewide applauded their efforts and portrayed them in a positive light—as sincere reformers whose interests were the will of the people rather than "bossism." Most importantly, the affair established Roosevelt as an up-and-coming leader in the party whose name increasingly was being linked with progressive reform. Just as his Republican cousin Theodore had reached great heights as a Progressive, now the younger Roosevelt, in the rival party, was carrying the torch of reform. As would so often be the case throughout his career, even political defeat could prove beneficial in the long run.

The struggle with Tammany set the tone for the remainder of Roosevelt's first term in office. Although he had been defeated, he established himself as a leader of the progressive wing of the Democratic party in New York, which might yield dividends in the future. Furthermore, the battle had taught him important lessons about the give-and-take of politics. One could be motivated by high ideals, but they had to be tempered by negotiation and a dose of realism. In fact, the more he worked alongside those legislators tied to the machine, the more he may have come to realize that New York politics was more complex than simply a morality play of the good reformers pitched in combat against an evil cabal centered in the city. He gradually began to form good working relations with several Tammany colleagues in the senate.

He also learned that at times Tammany even could be an important ally. Roosevelt sought to develop an image of himself as a representative of the common man, a natural goal for any politician whose constituency tended to be composed of rural farmers. The reality was that, while he might oppose Tammany's methods, there was no denying that the machine often was a voice for the blue-collar workers. The ring relied on the votes of New York's workingmen, particularly the growing immigrant population, which meant that in most cases any political leader hoping to cater to workers had to build positive relations with it. Given the size and the rate of growth of New York's working class, Roosevelt had to recognize that working with Tammany was crucial to establishing his credentials as a pro-labor Democrat.

Labor turned out to be one of Roosevelt's greatest challenges during his early years in government, probably for two reasons. One had to do with the composition of his congressional district, which was overwhelmingly agricultural. While workers in the cities and farmers in upstate New York at times supported the same measures, usually their views diverged. The other factor simply may have been Roosevelt's own background. Growing up as a patrician in Hyde Park gave him little connection with modest farmers, but he tended to identify with them much more than industrial workers in the cities. During his campaign, he enjoyed meeting with farmers in small towns in his district; he seldom had contact with large numbers of workers. Playing the role of a statewide progressive would take considerable political acumen, and Roosevelt exhibited a great deal of it during his first term. He successfully straddled the fence on labor issues, taking care to show his inclinations as a pro-labor progressive while maintaining his base of support among rural New Yorkers.

His early record on labor issues was not strong. He managed to earn an honorary appointment in the state branch of the Association for Labor Legislation, an important organization nationally that counted in its leadership such notable figures as American Federation of Labor head Samuel Gompers, the famed settlement house reformer Jane Addams, and progressive attorney (and later Supreme Court Justice) Louis Brandeis. He backed workers compensation legislation and on several occasions crossed over to the Tammany side of the senate floor to support labor bills. Perhaps most notably, Roosevelt played a pivotal role in winning passage of a law that limited the work week to 54 hours for many workers. The bill came very close to being defeated but survived due to his willingness to filibuster for hours until the party was able to bring enough votes together to get the measure approved.

There were limits, however, to Roosevelt's support for labor. Reflecting the values of his district, he opposed strikes and boycotts promoted by labor organizations. In high-profile labor boycott cases that reached the Supreme Court, Roosevelt sided with the state, believing that such practices only served to hinder production. He had little positive to say regarding strikes; on one occasion he supported a plan to strengthen the National Guard in New York, notable because at that time its primary role had been to suppress strike activity. While Roosevelt hardly could be considered a champion of the working man, he was successful in avoiding harsh criticism from the labor wing of the Democratic party. Labor issues would continue to challenge Roosevelt throughout his career.

In other areas, Roosevelt's status as a progressive was more evident. Perhaps based on his early battles with the Tammany machine, he was a vocal proponent of electoral reform, which was a central issue for the Progressive movement nationally. The main point of criticism that reformers had with U.S. democracy was that there was not enough of it. Progressive rhetoric, borrowing from the Populist insurgents of the late nineteenth century, which pitted big business and finance against farmers, often portrayed the U.S. political system as dominated by special interests. While individuals could use the ballot as a check on entrenched power, the argument ran that once in office, leaders could easily become corrupted. This mistrust of politicians was translated into a number of proposals that sought to bring political power closer to the people. Among them were the referendum and recall, which had caught on in many Western states and now were gaining popularity in other parts of the country. Allowing voters to intervene directly into the legislative process, many Progressives believed, would bring government closer to the masses.

Another area of Progressive electoral reform, of course, had to do with the election of United States senators. The United States Constitution had designed the Senate as the upper house of the bicameral legislature. The people, it was determined, would vote directly for representatives into the lower house; duly elected leaders in various states would have the responsibility of selecting members of the upper house. The design of the Senate reflected the view of the late-eighteenth-century founders that mass democracy had to be balanced by placing some power into the hands of the well-to-do and talented. In most states, the method for electing senators was to give that power to one or both houses of the state legislature. This had been the case in New York, where the state senate had such authority.

Views regarding this concept of limited democracy had been changing for decades, beginning as early as the 1820s and gradually gaining momentum. Increasing support for mass democracy went hand-in-hand with reform voices claiming that politicians could not be trusted once elected to office. State assemblies, reformers had been arguing for decades, were hotbeds of corruption and abuse of power. The United States Senate, under this logic, was the creation of entrenched power in legislatures across the land. Allowing the people to elect senators, just as they elected members of the House of Representatives, would bring the senator more closely in line with the will of the people.

Whether Roosevelt considered electoral reform before he arrived in the New York assembly was unclear. However, almost as soon as he stepped on the floor of the statehouse he began to be a vocal supporter of direct elections. He also promoted, quite vigorously, a bill that would transform the way in which candidates for office would be chosen within the party. In many states, parties continued to choose candidates through closed caucuses, where party leaders would be responsible for determining a slate of candidates for an election. Progressives had opened up the idea of a direct primary, where voters would go to the polls to select candidates for office. Roosevelt became a leader of the reformers, in both parties, who advocated a direct primary system for New York. During his first term, a bill that opened up the nominating process passed the legislature.

Another issue was women's suffrage, which by the early 1900s already had a decades-long history of debate. As with other controversies,

Roosevelt had to balance his own inclinations with the views of constituents in his home district. During the first months of his first term, he vacillated on the question, attempting to find a neutral position that would not alienate rural voters but also did not damage his reputation as a reformer. On one occasion, he argued that he would seek out the views of people in Dutchess County, rather than follow his own beliefs, and claimed that he would "be guided very largely by the result." On another occasion, he made the point again by stating that he was not opposed to women's suffrage, but that the people of New York should determine the matter, not the legislature. For committed proponents of reform, particularly those suffragists who had worked for decades to win support for a new law, such statements came across as somewhat empty. Over the following year, seeking to feel the pulse of the public, he gradually came around to supporting a law extending the right to vote to women.

Another challenge was Prohibition, a cause that had swept across the nation over several decades and resulted in many states adopting dry laws. Roosevelt found safe ground in "local option," arguing that the best policy was to allow locals to decide the matter for themselves. The urban elements of the Democratic party were strongly against any measure that would block the sale of alcohol; Roosevelt knew that supporting Prohibition would cause him difficulty with voters in New York City and once again bring on the wrath of Tammany. In the end, Roosevelt found a way to avoid political damage on the issue. In 1913, he introduced a bill, supported by the Anti-Saloon League, to allow cities to adopt their own policies with respect to the sale and consumption of alcohol. Even years later, when as president Roosevelt oversaw the repeal of the Eighteenth Amendment, which had made the sale of alcoholic beverages anywhere in the nation a federal offense, he was able to also claim that he had supported the cause of Prohibition while in the state senate.

These examples of political nuance at times were punctuated by causes for which Roosevelt seemed to be guided more by his own convictions, regardless of the political response. On the matter of conservation, not only did he confront Tammany directly, but he was able to reorient his party. Undoubtedly, Theodore Roosevelt, who during and after his presidency had worked to establish himself as America's preeminent conservationist, was a strong influence on him on this front. The younger Roosevelt's role in the conservationist movement, which began immediately upon entering the legislature, perhaps was something of a surprise. Very little in his years at Harvard or Groton indicated that he had even a passing interest in environmental issues. Yet by the end of his first term, Roosevelt had to be considered among the most vocal proponents of conservation in the assembly, and certainly within his own party.

As chairman of the senate's Forest, Fish, and Game Committee, his first major project was to block a bill that called for a relaxation on game hunting restrictions. His efforts met with failure, as the bill passed through the committee and was approved by the full senate. On other matters, Roosevelt was dogged in his support for strengthening environmental regulations, at times even coming to blows with his own party. Among the most notable efforts on this front had to do with a bill designed to protect forests from increased cutting. Sensing broad support for the measure, Roosevelt pushed the envelope by including restrictions on the cutting of timber not only on public lands, but also on privately owned property. Even some of his fellow conservationists questioned the constitutionality of such a measure; eventually this part of the bill was eliminated.

Despite his energetic work on the committee, his overall record on conservation was, on the whole, rather modest—more due to his inability to win victories on the senate floor than from a lack of conviction. Many of his proposals, like the logging restrictions that went down in defeat, were eviscerated before they passed through the legislature. During Roosevelt's tenure on the committee, New York passed few bills that altered government policy significantly with respect to natural resources or the environment. As with other matters, however, Roosevelt boosted his image as a reformer who was willing to take the fight directly to Tammany.

All of this activity during his first years in the state senate meant that Roosevelt had made a name for himself statewide in a short period of time. Some observers, both political colleagues and reporters, had begun to rally behind him as the future standard-bearer of the party, both in New York and nationally. Others found a great deal to criticize about the upstart politician. For some, his earnestness came across as self-righteousness; often he showed little ability to negotiate and seemed to lack nuance on issues. His remarkable confidence and willingness to take the reins of leadership as a rather young and inexperienced legislator also generated comments that he was arrogant—a view that at times was not unwarranted. Frances Perkins, a lobbyist for social reform in the state assembly who years later would become an important part of Roosevelt's presidential cabinet, was less than impressed with the young man when meeting him for the first time, remarking on more than one occasion on his lofty views of himself.

Another charge leveled at Roosevelt was that he was more a showman than a committed reformer. Again, this sentiment reflects perceptions of his outspokenness, and at times brashness, at such a young age. Naturally, reporters were drawn to his famous name, which seemed to make it into the newspapers much more frequently than other state senators. In a telling moment, Robert F. Wagner, who at the time was serving as president pro tempore of the senate, made the comment after Roosevelt had won an argument on the senate floor that "Senator Roosevelt has gained his point. What he wants is a headline in the newspapers." Such charges were perhaps exaggerated, but there was a grain of truth in them. He was ambitious and sought to use his position in the legislature as a springboard to higher office.

By the end of his first term in office, he had several achievements to which he could point. Without alienating voters in his rural district, he had done a remarkable job of appealing to a broader segment of New Yorkers. His brand of progressivism resonated more with supporters of Theodore Roosevelt than with his own party. A speech he delivered in Troy, New York, at a meeting of a reform group called the Peoples Forum offered a glimpse into his emerging political philosophy. He told his listeners that much of the American past had been driven by competition, but that now the nation had entered into a new age—one that called for more cooperation, or what he called a "struggle for liberty of the community rather than the liberty of the individual." This new way of thinking, he explained, was necessary to address the inefficiency and limitations of unbridled individualism in a highly industrialized society.

Most striking about the speech was that these sentiments were almost identical to those made only weeks before by Theodore Roosevelt, who was seeking another term as president under the banner of the Progressive, or "Bull Moose," party. Teddy's slogan for these ideas was the "New Nationalism," an attempt to distinguish his own views from that of Progressive Democrats led primarily by Woodrow Wilson. Franklin described his conservation efforts as an example of this new ethos in government; when he made these comments, one probably could almost hear his cousin's voice. Even more consistent with Theodore's New Nationalism were Franklin's comments on corporate monopolies, which had become a major issue for both parties. Theodore had made a name for himself as a "trust buster," willing to use presidential power to eradicate dangerous combinations in business and industry. The elder Roosevelt's views on monopoly had evolved, however, and gradually he came to the view that monopolies would best be managed through regulation rather than dissolution. Instead of attacking monopolies on moral grounds, as the Populists had done in the late nineteenth century, New Nationalists promoted the idea that a new spirit of cooperation and management would eliminate the excesses of monopoly but retain the attributes of highly complex businesses. In words that could have been drawn directly from a speech made by Theodore Roosevelt, Franklin told the Troy audience that "the mere size of a trust is not of necessity its evil. The trust is evil because it monopolizes for a few and as long as this keeps up it will be necessary for a community to change its features."

If he was guilty of sounding too much like Theodore Roosevelt, one could understand his reasoning. The Bull Moose party seemed to be gaining steam, particularly in states with a strong Progressive element such as New York. Franklin no doubt agreed with his mentor on these issues; however, he also understood the direction of the political winds, in his home state and nationally. He seemed to be achieving what any aspirant to national office sought: popularity that transcended party lines. As the election year of 1912 moved forward, it was clear that he was at least as much interested in events in Washington as he was those in Albany, perhaps even more so.

Roosevelt plunged into the 1912 election season with the enthusiasm that had come to mark his career. He actually had two campaigns to consider—the presidential election and also his own reelection bid—and as it turned out he worked more on the former. In the end, both were successful, and the year turned out to be pivotal both for the Democratic party and particularly for Roosevelt.

His role in Woodrow Wilson's campaign was limited to activities in New York, but Roosevelt did everything he could to carry the state for his party. Evidence suggests that his energies were somewhat self-serving, for he understood that a victory for Wilson might result in Roosevelt winning an appointment in the new administration. He had met Wilson, and the two seemed to hit it off well, and the Wilson team had to be aware of this rising star in such an important state. One indication of his yearning for an opportunity to work in Washington was his reluctance to run for reelection in the state senate. A few voices in the party had thrown out his name as a possibility for the governorship of New York, an unrealistic goal for someone who only recently had reached the minimum age for the office. He pondered his future throughout the summer of 1912, all the while watching the ongoing presidential campaign.

Ultimately, he decided to run for reelection, but the campaign was not exactly the high point of his career. He contracted typhoid fever in September, only a month after receiving the nomination for the seat. Unable to run an active campaign as he had before, there was a good chance he would go down in defeat, considering that his victory was a narrow one in 1910 and that the Republicans were determined to make a comeback following their poor statewide showing that year. While he might have been ambivalent about the job, he also understood that an electoral defeat early in his career could be a serious setback.

Once again, Roosevelt was the beneficiary of good fortune, this time in meeting Louis McHenry Howe, a newspaper reporter who had been following Roosevelt's career while writing for the New York *Herald*. Howe had written positively about Roosevelt on several occasions during his first term and held the freshman legislator in high regard. The relationship that began in the summer of 1912 would last for more than two decades. Not only did Howe play a crucial role in Roosevelt's reelection bid; he also became a key assistant for him throughout much of his career.

The two men could not have been more different in almost every way. Roosevelt, a handsome, tall man, struck an almost regal appearance, while Howe was short and often had an unkempt appearance. Roosevelt had grown up in an affluent environment and would always be financially secure; Howe always seemed to live on the margins. Roosevelt was an idealistic, enthusiastic politician who seemed to see most issues in black and white. Howe was at heart a political strategist, concerning himself less with the merits of particular issues and more with the game of political maneuvering. Together, the two would merge their talents to become a formidable team.

What attracted Howe to Roosevelt initially is unclear. He may have agreed with Roosevelt's reform ideas, but he also had to have been drawn to the man because of his potential stardom. Their first meetings had been in the summer of 1912, while New York Democrats had been engaged in heated debate over delegate selection for the upcoming presidential convention. They must have hit it off well, because by the end of the summer, Howe, having trouble finding sustained work, had contacted Roosevelt about the upcoming senate campaign. When Roosevelt became ill, he immediately called on Howe and asked him to manage his campaign while Roosevelt recovered in bed.

Howe worked tirelessly for Roosevelt and was a decisive factor in winning reelection. He visited virtually every inch of the district, encouraging Roosevelt supporters to carry his campaign message to the broader public. In a move that became one of Howe's trademarks, he spent as much time behind the scenes with party leaders, believing that the path to political success began within the party, not on the stump. He also paid close attention to the makeup of Roosevelt's district, formulating a campaign message aimed at farmers that seemed to herald back to the Populist era by pitting them against corporate moguls and their cronies in the legislature.

Even with Howe's efforts, the election was not a foregone conclusion, and Roosevelt won by the narrowest of margins. However, the victory was noteworthy, considering that he had been unable to campaign as actively as in the first campaign. Furthermore, the district still counted more Republicans than Democrats, and the Republican party had performed well statewide. Roosevelt was aware of the valuable role Howe had played and had no intentions of running another campaign without him.

Roosevelt's second term in office was brief. His most notable work had to do with a series of agricultural bills he had proposed, in many respects as an attempt to follow up on promises he (and Howe) had made during the campaign. Several of the measures met with intense opposition, and beginning in January Roosevelt found himself embroiled in hearings over the legislation as opponents, particularly representatives of merchants who argued that some of the regulations would cut into their livelihood, sought to derail these efforts.

But even as these intense debates were taking place, important events were happening outside New York. Wilson had won the presidency in November, and already by the end of January Roosevelt was engaging in conversations with members of the incoming president's staff regarding a possible appointment in the new administration. Roosevelt very much wanted one and did his part to lobby on his own behalf over the next several weeks, a fact that people close to him, included Eleanor, admitted. Intentionally or unintentionally, Roosevelt had an encounter with incoming Secretary of the Navy Josephus Daniels while both men were in Washington for the inauguration in March. As Daniels later recalled, Roosevelt approached him in a hotel lobby to congratulate him on his appointment. Daniels, who had met Roosevelt the year before and had been impressed with him, immediately asked if he would be interested in becoming assistant secretary of the navy. Roosevelt responded enthusiastically; Daniels a few days later received approval from Wilson to offer the appointment. Roosevelt was headed for Washington.

Roosevelt's tenure in the New York Senate was brief but overwhelmingly successful. He had gained important experience, both in campaigning and in policymaking, and had learned a great deal about the ways in which political circles operated. He also had established himself as a well-known reformer across the state, and while he did not enjoy the fame of Theodore, he did have a generally positive reputation. He had, in fact, established himself as one of the more promising young politicians in the state. In later years, he would capitalize on this groundwork.

Chapter 3

WASHINGTON

Roosevelt saw Woodrow Wilson's triumph for exactly what it was—an opportunity to leap onto the national political stage. The new president, a former professor and president of Princeton University, had taken advantage of a split within the Republican party between progressives and conservatives and trounced his two opponents, receiving 435 electoral votes to Theodore Roosevelt's 88 (the incumbent William Howard Taft tallied only 8 votes). The victory emboldened Democrats nationwide, who believed the political tide had turned and that the era of Republican dominance in Washington had come to an end.

Wilson would now have the opportunity to launch a legislative campaign that followed the ideals of his progressive campaign slogan, the "New Freedom." The election had centered on the issue of corporate monopoly, as both he and Theodore Roosevelt sought to establish themselves as opponents of big business. If there was a difference between the two, it essentially may have been one of rhetoric. Roosevelt's "New Nationalism," based upon the ideas of his advisor and political writer Herbert Croly, took the point of view that monopolies were not, of necessity, evil. While they called for regulation, Wilson used a more populist tone in blasting "trusts" as counter to democracy and calling for their elimination.

Once in office, Wilson's reform program targeted several areas. Along with antimonopoly initiatives, the administration also sought a lowering of tariff rates and reform of the monetary system—issues that had been a part of the political landscape for many years. With the Democrats now controlling both houses of Congress, Wilson was poised to achieve legislative victories in all three areas. With respect to trusts, he oversaw the passage of the Clayton Antitrust Act, which allowed for stronger policing of "combinations in restraint of trade." He also approved the formation of a new government body, the Federal Trade Commission, which was designed to investigate and file charges against such monopolies.

On the matter of tariffs, Wilson's election brought about the culmination of Democratic efforts to lower import duties that dated back to at least the 1890s, a move that was popular with farmers and agricultural interests. Along with this action, which would decrease government revenue, Americans witnessed the ratification of the Sixteenth Amendment, which provided for a national income tax. By the end of Wilson's first year in office, the nation's currency system changed significantly through the creation of the Federal Reserve System. All of these reforms were accomplished early in Wilson's first term and represented significant turning points in U.S. government and economics.

Franklin Roosevelt supported Wilson's New Freedom, although philosophically he was closer to cousin Theodore. However, during the early years of the Wilson administration, Roosevelt was focused directly on his duties at the Navy Department. Military matters took a back seat to Wilson's domestic reform agenda, which meant that for the time being Roosevelt was not in the limelight. This would change after 1914, when Europe plunged into World War I. Between then and Roosevelt's arrival in Washington, he learned a great deal about the navy and about Washington politics.

Roosevelt was only 31 years old when sworn in as assistant secretary of the navy and had only three years of experience in politics. He was the youngest man to have ever held the position; his boss, Secretary of the Navy Josephus Daniels, was 20 years older. Most of the commanders and officials who fell under Roosevelt's authority also were much older, and at times this was a problem for him. On more than one occasion, he was subject to ribbing by those around him as being a "little boy." Nevertheless, in characteristic Roosevelt fashion, he was undaunted by his lack of experience and plunged into the job with enthusiasm and confidence.

Not surprisingly, Roosevelt found the hustle and bustle of Washington professional and social life to his liking. The family moved into a modest but elegant house on N Street in the heart of the city, close enough for Franklin to walk to his office at the Navy Department. Both he and Eleanor quickly entered the Washington social scene, a world that Franklin seemed to relish and that Eleanor tolerated. The job demanded a great deal of Roosevelt's time, as he worked full days and attended official and semi-official gatherings on many evenings each week. Eleanor and the children saw less and less of him.

Social life in Washington was not foreign to the Roosevelts, who had visited there on many occasions and already knew many people working in and around the government. As members of New York and Boston high society, they had little difficulty entering the environment, a transition that many newcomers to Washington found very challenging. Franklin was comfortable in this world, dining regularly at the posh Metropolitan Club, frequenting the exclusive golf clubs where as much policymaking occurred as in administrative offices, and enjoying the finer restaurants in the evenings. He once described Washington society as "the saloon, the salon, and the Salome." Saloons were those gathering places where drink was plentiful; salons were noted for their sophisticated crowds and conversation. Salomes were gatherings in the finer homes in the city, known for their refinement. Roosevelt came to love all three.

Eleanor, for her part, carried out her responsibilities as wife of a high-ranking public servant dutifully. She also was a full-time mother, as Franklin had little to do with the rearing of the children. At times they would visit his office, and he tried to spend time with them in the evenings. For the most part, though, the children saw their father as a distant, albeit affectionate, parent. Eleanor also was expected to be something of a social secretary for the couple, arranging parties and dinners for members of their social circle. She was not uncomfortable with the role, considering her background, but the work could be quite demanding. She also found such responsibilities unfulfilling. During these years, she somehow found the time and energy to become involved in reform causes, which became her trademark in later years. She was not merely a housewife, for oftentimes visitors remarked that she advised her husband on matters of policy. Those close to the Roosevelts often described Eleanor as an anchor for her husband, reminding him of appointments and serving as a voice of stability. Given Franklin's breezy, perhaps even whimsical, persona, the two made a good team.

Early on, Eleanor attempted to carry out all of these duties alone. Her schedule must have been overwhelming, as each day she alternated between caring for the children and attending to the demands of Washington society. According to one story, Eleanor made 60 social calls in one week alone. Eventually, she hired a social secretary to assist her, an attractive, vivacious 23-year-old woman perfectly suited for the role, Lucy Page Mercer. She was the daughter of a socially connected family, which meant she understood the protocols of Washington social and professional life. Everyone in the family became quite fond of her. The children later remembered her as friendly and upbeat, Eleanor found her indispensable, and Franklin beamed when he encountered the "lovely Lucy." Even

Franklin's mother Sara, always watching over the family, took a liking to Mercer.

Roosevelt's relationship with his new boss was amiable but never very warm. The two men struck quite a contrast. Daniels, a North Carolinian with a southern disposition, had made a name for himself as a populist reformer more in the mold of William Jennings Bryan than Woodrow Wilson. He was an interesting selection as secretary of the navy, as he often displayed isolationist tendencies and on occasion referred to himself as a pacifist. His appointment, along with the selection of the isolationist Bryan as secretary of state, was an indication that foreign policy was not the central focus of Wilson's presidency. Roosevelt's initial reaction to this soft-spoken and oftentimes disheveled southerner is unclear, but a remark he made years later was telling in that he recalled thinking that Daniels was "the funniest looking hill-billy I had ever seen."

Daniels may have looked like a hayseed, but as it turned out he did not play the part. He proved to be a shrewd and decisive leader who earned the trust and admiration of most people around him, including Roosevelt. Although slow in his movement and mannerisms, and deliberate in his decision-making, he set clear boundaries and made it clear to subordinates that he was the navy's civilian leader. This attitude alone may have been the source of some friction with Roosevelt, whose aspirations were lofty. After all, it had been his mentor and idol Theodore Roosevelt who had used the position of assistant secretary of the navy to launch himself into fame, overstepping the authority of his superior when basically sparking the Spanish-American War while his boss had been away from the office. Franklin once mentioned the event to a reporter, perhaps only half-joking: "You remember what happened the last time a Roosevelt occupied a similar position."

Daniels, however, was not one to be overstepped. His conservative approach to leadership, along with a firmness of resolve, was a good fit with Roosevelt; the two men developed an effective professional relationship. In fact, these differences in personality may have served the navy well. Daniels—cautious, fiscally conservative, and with an eye for detail— was an excellent administrator who lacked enthusiasm for military life. Roosevelt had lofty visions for the navy and continually commented on the need to increase its size and budget. Daniels was good with numbers and details but not great with people. Roosevelt was the opposite; he became bored when confronted with statistics but enjoyed dealing with people. Daniels preferred to wait before making decisions, opting to gather as much evidence and thinking problems through. Roosevelt tended to rely on instinct and was always ready to launch new plans. The fact that these two men, given their differences, not only worked well together but came to admire one another was a credit to both of them.

Although Roosevelt clearly would be second in command, he did have several responsibilities and contributed a great deal to the running of the navy. He proved to have an exceptional ability to juggle various administrative and political responsibilities. Part of the reason he was able to do so many things simultaneously was that he insisted on bringing the indispensable Louis Howe to Washington with him to serve as his personal secretary. Howe seemed to be everywhere at once, assisting Roosevelt in all matters—scheduling appointments, helping with clerical work, and even helping Roosevelt keep an eye on, and a hand in, New York politics. Daniels described him as "one of the strangest men I have ever met and one of the smartest." There was no questioning his loyalty to Roosevelt. Daniels on another occasion marveled that Howe "would have laid on the floor and let Franklin walk over him." Certainly Howe was committed to advancing Roosevelt's career.

Roosevelt's primary jobs were to oversee all civilian personnel in the navy and to keep track of budgets and contracts. Daniels, despite his firm leadership, allowed him considerable autonomy, which meant that Roosevelt did have considerable power; many of his predecessors in the position had much less authority. If the job seemed a little mundane to him early on, it soon became much more intense as Europe began to plunge into war. Although the Wilson administration pledged neutrality from the outset, certainly U.S. military policy would have to respond to world events.

Early in his tenure in the Navy Department, Roosevelt's most significant responsibilities had to do with labor negotiations with defense contractors. In the area of labor, Roosevelt gained valuable experience that helped him in later years. By working with labor leaders and having direct contact with workers in the defense industry, he gained an appreciation for labor issues and learned how to navigate the sometimes rocky waters of labor disputes. His primary goal in this area was to encourage positive relations between workers, industry leaders, and the military—not a small task given their differing agendas.

One conflict that was already brewing when Roosevelt arrived in Washington had to do with attempts to increase efficiency in naval yards. Cutting costs had been a goal of the Taft administration, and the conservative Daniels applauded any reforms that might increase productivity without raising costs. In particular, the navy had begun considering the adoption of the Taylor system in its production plants. Named after engineer Frederick Winslow Taylor, who pioneered the principles in the steel industry in the late nineteenth century, the idea revolved around increasing worker productivity by streamlining the various tasks involved in manufacturing. Taylor's studies had emphasized, among other things, the need to study the motions of workers in an assembly line, calculating ways to speed up the amount of production each worker could achieve in a given time. Over the next two decades, several industries had adopted Taylorist concepts, sparking opposition by labor organizations who saw the philosophy as one that dehumanized individual workers.

While union leaders claimed that Taylorism was a means of exploiting workers with flimsy theories, for progressive reformers these principles presented a dilemma. On one hand, many did find something distasteful in a philosophy that approached workers as little more than statistical data—seeming to suggest that the economy was based on calculations that focused on the bottom line rather than the treatment of individuals. However, Taylorism appealed to those attracted by its scientific approach to questions of labor and productivity. If a commitment to improving the conditions of workers was a central tenet of Progressive reform, the use of expert knowledge to improve efficiency in all aspects of life was another.

The conflict that had been brewing between labor and management in the private economy spilled over into the military when the War Department, during the Taft administration, elected to experiment with Taylorism in an armaments plant in New York. The results, in terms of productivity, had been positive, and plans were underway to expand these concepts to other defense-related plants. As Wilson entered the White House, labor advocates were lining up for a showdown.

Roosevelt entered his position in the midst of the growing controversy. He did everything he could to understand the issue by reading up on Taylorism and also meeting with labor representatives. The issue was important to him, for he entered the job with a view that he could bring more efficiency into naval production through reasoned reform. Early on in his tenure, eager to increase productivity and to make a name for himself, he brought in engineers and advisors, many of whom advocated these types of changes. Felix Frankfurter, a young and very bright attorney working in the War Department, provided Roosevelt with impressive evidence of the improvement that might be made in production through the adoption of Taylorism.

Yet there was a negative side, as Roosevelt also sensed the negative reaction such a decision would have with labor organizations and the bitter feuds that might erupt if such principles were adopted. The issue ran the risk of becoming a serious political issue. For months he sought a way to placate both sides and also please his superiors. That he was able to do so was another indication that Roosevelt possessed an impressive political acumen. Stating that he would never allow any system to be "imposed from above on an unwilling working force," a comment that brought cheers from labor, he nevertheless committed the navy to a continued search for efficiency-increasing measures. This evasive, middle-of-the-road approach did one thing for Roosevelt—it bought him time. Within a year, Congress had taken up the issue and eventually passed a bill that barred the implementation of Taylorism in any defense industry. While Roosevelt may not have displayed bold leadership, he had learned that in times of polarized dispute the best policy can be moderation.

Another responsibility Roosevelt faced was overseeing contracts between private industry and the Navy Department. Although he had little experience with labor before arriving in Washington, he was more comfortable with this role. He had worked as a corporate lawyer on Wall Street and understood the world of big business. In these matters there was a potential strain between Roosevelt and Daniels, who had made his name as a populist Democrat in North Carolina by fighting big business. Daniels had little experience with corporate moguls and had little interest in cultivating relationships with them. For the progressive southerner, businessmen were circumspect, and it was the job of the Navy Department to prevent corporations from bilking the government of revenue through bloated contracts.

Interestingly, Roosevelt adapted very readily to Daniel's sentiments. In what became something of a sport, the two men spent much time investigating contracts to root out waste. The office even made national headlines when Daniels rejected multiple, but identical, bids for steel plating for the construction of the new battleship *Arizona*. Daniels sensed collusion in the bidding and dispatched Roosevelt to negotiate with foreign steel manufacturers, a move designed to send a message to those U.S. companies that might be seeking to fix prices. The ploy worked. The U.S. companies issued new bids considerably lower than their initial offerings.

Roosevelt also became more sensitive to the issue of industrial partnerships and the potential for corporations to eliminate competition. He and Daniels fought energetically to break a hold on coal prices that they believed were fixed by a small group of mining companies. Although the outcome of the coal crusade was less than perfect (the Navy Department ended up purchasing a considerable amount of cheap, but very poor quality, coal), Roosevelt received good press for his willingness to promote competitive bidding in defense contracting. Although he never shared Daniels's visceral mistrust of corporate America, Roosevelt's experiences in contract negotiations may have influenced his views on the relationship between government and big business.

In most of these matters, Roosevelt and Daniels, despite their differences, were able to find common ground. Both were committed to making the Navy Department more efficient, and Daniels was pleased with Roosevelt's caution in dealing with labor. This amiable relationship was challenged, however, by fundamental disagreements with respect to foreign affairs and America's role in the world—a disagreement that existed throughout the Wilson administration. Their disagreements mattered little before the outbreak of World War I, but they did indicate that Roosevelt already had developed clear ideas regarding U.S. military power and diplomacy. Two issues emerged in the early years of Roosevelt's naval career that illustrated the divergence between his views and those of his superior.

The first centered on relations with Japan. The state legislature of California recently had passed an "alien land bill" that prevented Japanese immigrants from owning land in the state. The measure created a firestorm of reaction in Japan. The government in Tokyo issued a strong statement that called the act "unfair and discriminatory" and implied that the law might lead to a revision of treaties between the two nations. Throughout Japan the reaction was even more heated as mobs took to the streets in protest of the law. A meeting of the Joint Board of the Army and Navy, an advisory group of high-ranking commanders, concluded that the rift had the potential to become a serious matter. A few voices even stated that war between the two countries was imminent, as they believed the Japanese government was using the controversy to whip up support for a military invasion of the Philippines and perhaps the Hawaiian Islands.

Daniels, true to form, rejected these bellicose voices and called for caution. For one thing, he spoke out against those officers in the army who seemed intent on influencing decision-making in the navy. He also refuted every argument for aggressive actions in the Pacific that might lead to war, such as moving U.S. ships docked in China to Manila Bay. He and Secretary of State Bryan, both avowed moderates in foreign policy, acted quickly to convince the president to ignore those who promoted confrontation with Japan.

Roosevelt was not part of these inner-circle meetings, but he clearly came down on the side of army commanders and others who called for a response to Japan's aggressive language. On several occasions he discussed in private the possibilities of an impending war and criticized the efforts of his boss to dismiss the Joint Board's recommendations. Yet he also showed restraint, taking care to avoid speaking publicly against his superior or the president so as to avoid controversy. While the administration managed to speak with one voice and elected to downplay the Japanese reaction, the crisis was the first indication that Roosevelt and Daniels were far apart on matters of defense. With respect to the California law, Roosevelt sat quietly while the administration pointed to states' rights as the reasoning behind Washington's unwillingness to seek a change in the policy. Roosevelt again disagreed.

In the case of the revolutionary upheaval in Mexico, Roosevelt's enthusiasm for a more aggressive naval policy became even more evident. The problems had begun during the Taft administration, when revolutionary activity bubbling beneath the surface of dictator Porfirio Diaz's Mexico finally erupted into violence in 1911. In the early stages of the revolution, a middle-class and pro-democratic reformer named Francisco Madero emerged as the leader of a new government in Mexico City. When Wilson entered the White House, he embraced Madero as the legitimate leader of the country. His hold on power, however, was short-lived; in February 1913, military strongman Victorian Huerta led his forces into the capital and ousted Madero. Both men claimed to be the leader of Mexico, and Wilson faced a difficult challenge.

From the outset, Wilson's foreign policy team was divided on how to proceed with respect to Mexico. Bryan, along with Daniels, operated on the assumption that Mexico's political crisis was not an American problem. They called for restraint in Washington and a policy of neutrality. Wilson, however, had been outraged by Huerta's coup. In what would become a trademark of Wilson's foreign policy, he began to suggest that the United States had a commitment to promote democracy in Mexico and very much wanted to see the military government ousted. Tensions increased when U.S. sailors docked at the port city of Tampico and were arrested by Huerta's troops. Although Huerta had no desire to anger the United States and quickly released the men with an apology, the incident gave pro-interventionists ammunition.

Relations between the two countries became more strained in April 1914, when news reached Washington that a German ship carrying weapons had arrived at Vera Cruz to sell to Huerta's government. Wilson acted immediately, dispatching U.S. troops to Mexico with orders to seize the armaments. A firefight resulted, leaving 19 U.S. soldiers dead. A large-scale military intervention in Mexico seemed imminent.

Roosevelt contributed to these calls for war and did everything he could to prepare for it. He contacted naval commanders stationed in the Pacific and readied them for deployment—shades of his uncle's actions when he manned the same desk—and made several public comments indicating that the United States Navy was ready for war. Daniels, however, had no intention of seeing his subordinate seize the initiative; he and Bryan won the day by convincing Wilson to hold off on immediate retaliation. As time passed, so too did the crisis. Huerta was eventually overthrown, and the new government in Mexico, led by the civilian Venustiano Carranza, called on all U.S. troops to leave the country. With Huerta out of power, any support for war in the United States waned as intervention would be viewed as an overstepping of U.S. responsibilities.

Wilson instead elected to offer mediation between the rival groups in Mexico, which included Carranza, Huerta, and others. Roosevelt was uncompromising in his view that the United States had a role to play in Mexico, even speaking publicly about a growing American "war spirit" while administration officials were seeking a peaceful end to the conflict. He even implied in one public address that annexation of Mexico was not altogether out of the question.

Roosevelt would have to wait for his war, but not for long. Wilson, accurately assessing public opinion and following the advice of moderates, pulled the United States away from the brink. Theodore Roosevelt, who had chided the administration's foreign policy from the outset, sat on the sidelines and complained of Wilson's weakness. His younger relative agreed with the assessment but was in no position to alter the dispositions of his superiors. Yet even as this crisis was unfolding, much more turbulent events were taking place in Europe. Soon the nations of Europe would be at war, and eventually the United States would join them. Roosevelt would be a key contributor to the war effort.

Chapter 4

AT WAR

"Heir to Austrian Throne Is Slain with His Wife by a Bosnian Youth To Avenge Seizure of His Country." The *New York Times* headline of June 29, 1914, generated little response in the United States. Violence had become quite commonplace in the Balkan region of Europe over the past few decades, and this latest incident indicated that perhaps another wave of upheaval was beginning. Those who continued reading the story would learn that the Austrian government had declared its outrage by the crime and certainly would retaliate. While ominous in tone, the news fell on deaf ears. Most Americans could not point out Sarajevo, the Bosnian city where the attack occurred, on a map. War might indeed break out between the Austro-Hungarian Empire and the nation-state of Serbia. If so, it would be simply another conflict in the region.

There was, however, a worst-case scenario, which turned out to be far worse than even those who were knowledgeable about the region could have expected. The avalanche of events pushing toward a widespread European war were experienced in the United States with a combination of confusion and bewilderment. The events happened so rapidly that even the nation's leaders could not keep up with them. Russia, under the rule of Tsar Nicholas II, mobilized troops on the Austrian border and threatened war if the Emperor of Austria decided to invade Serbia (the Austrians believed the Serbian government to be complicit in the assassination). Within a week a larger war seemed to be imminent.

Roosevelt, who had been vacationing at Campobello during the crisis, returned to Washington with a sense of urgency but found the mood to be calm, perhaps even complacent. During the next few days, negotiations between the European powers became almost surreal. Germany's government, a strong ally of Austria, issued a series of ultimatums to Russia. The Kaiser then confronted France, declaring that the government in Paris had less than 24 hours to make clear whether that country planned to come to the aid of Russia if war began.

Troubled by these events, Roosevelt left Washington on August 1 for Reading, Pennsylvania, to speak at a dedicatory ceremony for an anchor of the U.S.S. *Maine*, the famous vessel that in 1898 had exploded off the coast of Cuba and launched the Spanish-American War. As he was returning from the event, he received word that Germany had declared war on Russia. Soon France and England would enter the fray, thus beginning the most destructive war in the history of humankind.

While the news seemed to come with dizzying speed, the seeds of World War I actually had been planted years before. The powers of Europe were gripped in the vice of a treaty system developed in the prior century. The most ominous of these was the so-called Dual Alliance between the Kaiser's Germany and the Austro-Hungarian Empire. As Germany's relations with Russia soured in the 1890s, the Tsar turned to France as a means to check this growing power bloc in Central Europe. Many observers described this arrangement as an effort to assure "balance" in conflict-ridden Europe. The thinking was that a system of treaties meant that no single country would encourage war because of the protections guaranteed by such agreements. There was, of course, a more pessimistic view of the system—that the treaty system all but guaranteed that an otherwise isolated conflict would erupt into a larger war if countries met their commitments.

Germany's actions seemed the most troubling. Kaiser Wilhelm II had overseen a frenzied militarization of that country beginning in the 1890s to strengthen its position. A romantic sense of nationalism among the German people, which flourished in the late nineteenth century, evolved into an aggressive militancy that not only encouraged visions of grandeur for a German empire but also fueled mistrust, even hostility, toward other Europeans. The German military's high command, always forward-looking, had for years prior to 1914 contemplated a glorious war that would bring about a reordering of the European political landscape and usher in an era of greatness for the country.

Germany's long-range military strategy had a tremendous impact on the way World War I began. The original architect was the Baron Alfred von Schlieffen, who years earlier had responded to the Kaiser's fears of fighting a war on two fronts concurrently should conflict occur. The Schlieffen plan was both logical and sinister. If warfare seemed imminent, the plan required Germany to launch an invasion of France through neutral Belgium in order to avoid the stronger defenses France had placed along the German-French border. The unsuspecting French (not to mention the Belgians) would be overrun and defeated so that Germany could then confront Russia in the East. For years the plan was theoretical; however, as Russian troops headed for the Austrian border, threatening Germany's ally, the German high command made the plan a reality. Within days of declaring war of Russia, a massive German force crashed its way through Belgium with its sights set on Paris.

The final step in this conflagration was England's response to Germany's aggressions. On August 3, an ultimatum left London for Berlin calling for immediate withdrawal of German troops from Belgium. The leadership in Germany sneered; one official marveled that England would be willing to go to war over a "scrap of paper"—a reference to an agreement made years ago in which the British guaranteed Belgian neutrality. The following day, England declared war on Germany. Two days later, Austria declared war on Russia. The "Great War" of Europe had begun.

President Wilson's reaction to these events was clear and firm—the United States would not be a part of the conflict. The very day that England declared war on Germany, Wilson issued a proclamation of neutrality. The president, grief-stricken by the death of his wife Ellen, was in complete agreement with Secretary of State Bryan and Secretary of the Navy Daniels, who both advised that the United States should take no action that might be construed as an intention of taking a side in the conflict.

Not everyone in Washington agreed with Wilson's sentiments, including Roosevelt. The General Board, the primary military body involved with strategy, recommended a new program of defense preparedness. The war might be in Europe, these voices claimed, but could very rapidly engulf the Western Hemisphere. Furthermore, there was a fear that U.S. ships on the high seas might be at risk. In the initial months of the war, Roosevelt received messages from several high-ranking military officials pointing out a need for a new defense strategy. Among the more notable episodes was a letter he received from Admiral Alfred Thayer Mahan, the elderly dean of U.S. naval strategy who had influenced the development of the U.S. navy perhaps more than any individual in the history of the nation. Now retired and declining in health, his words must have had an impact on Roosevelt. He pleaded for action and explained that "I write to you because I know of no one else in the Administration to whom I should care to write." The letter only further reinforced in Roosevelt's mind that his ideas regarding naval strategy were being drowned out by his superiors.

These disagreements between Roosevelt and Daniels had become a pattern. In prior instances Roosevelt had displayed loyalty by keeping his views to himself. Now, however, with the stakes so high in his mind, the conflict tore at him. To complicate matters even more, Wilson, aware of the growing criticism around him, issued orders that no one down the chain of command should make public comments regarding the war or national defense policy. Once again, Roosevelt found himself in a difficult position, and at times he violated the desires of the administration. While he and Daniels continued to maintain amicable relations, the strain was showing. Daniels would imply in his memoirs years later that he considered asking Roosevelt to step down out of concern that his assistant's grandstanding might generate a political circus. Daniels showed restraint. Roosevelt did his best to do the same.

To Roosevelt's credit, he did find ways of expressing his frustrations while at the same time avoiding direct conflict with the president. On several occasions he made public remarks on the need for a strong defense while avoiding specific questions regarding the war. He testified before a House Naval Affairs Committee and discussed the need for a larger and better-equipped navy but refused to criticize Wilson. During the session he was asked to comment directly on Wilson's war policy. Hesitating, and noting the throng of reporters in the room, he demurred. "It would not be my place," he observed, "to discuss matters of policy."

Privately, however, Roosevelt seethed. In several letters to Eleanor he blasted both Daniels and Bryan. "A complete smashup is inevitable, and there are a good many problems for us to consider," he wrote at the outset of the war. "Mr. D totally fails to grasp the situation." The fact that neither Daniels nor Bryan had military experience fed into Roosevelt's view that he knew better than they what the trajectory of naval policy should be. "Mr. Daniels," he wrote on another occasion, was "feeling chiefly very sad that his faith in human nature and civilization and similar idealistic nonsense was receiving." The invective continued. "These dear good people like W.J.B. and J.D. have as much conception of what a general European war means as Elliot [Roosevelt's young son] has of higher mathematics."

These barbs have been the subject of much writing by historians. Certainly they were an indication of Roosevelt's powerful ego and the exuberance of youth. At the same time, Roosevelt was not the only individual making such comments. In fact, the administration was being assaulted by

Republicans for what they described as a vacillating and ill-prepared strategy. More significantly, as the war moved into its second year, Wilson did begin to implement a policy of preparedness. When the president decided to form a committee to generate a set of plans, Roosevelt's name came up immediately. The fact that the war clearly was going to be a prolonged affair, combined with the need to confront the growing chant of criticism toward the administration, gradually moved military policy closer to Roosevelt's views.

Yet the changes that came were less than dramatic. Roosevelt arrived at the committee full of ideas that he urged the navy to adopt. One, of course, was a significant increase in naval production, particularly battleships and cruisers. He also promoted the creation of a naval reserve program in the event that global demands created strains on current military personnel. He also suggested the idea of forming a draft labor program in order to achieve rapid military buildup and also to promote a sense of national unity—a concept that never was adopted.

Roosevelt could point to some gains. He witnessed the creation of a reserve system, albeit more limited than he would have preferred. Procurement budgets were adjusted, but the dramatic change in weapons production that Roosevelt wanted did not take place. In fact, despite the views of Roosevelt and others within the military establishment, overall defense preparations remained minimal. Wilson understood that most Americans shared his noninterventionist sentiments. As the war pushed on into 1916, an election year for the president, he allowed the use of a phrase made during the Democratic Convention to become a major campaign slogan: He Kept Us Out of War. Roosevelt may have been disappointed by the caution exhibited by the administration, but it may have been the deciding factor in Wilson's reelection bid. He won a narrow victory over Charles Evans Hughes, the Republican candidate, largely due to his message that he had no intentions of entering the war.

While Wilson continued to chart a course of caution and neutrality, events continued to push the United States closer to intervention. The administration had already weathered several storms, such as the *Lusitania* incident, when on May 17, 1915, a German submarine sank a British passenger liner, killing over one thousand civilians, including 124 Americans. The tragedy emboldened those who were pushing for U.S. entry into the war and placed the administration on the defensive. An official apology from the Germans, and eventually the issuance of a declaration that unconditional submarine warfare would be suspended, bought the administration time. Following Wilson's reelection, events moved rapidly.

The German military command, seeking to turn the tide in a war that had stalemated, announced on February 1, 1917, that unrestricted submarine warfare would recommence. For Wilson, the new policy was an indication that negotiations with Germany had been a ruse, and most likely an effort to buy time.

Over the next several weeks those fears were confirmed by a harrowing sequence of events. In late February, British intelligence intercepted a telegram originating in Berlin that was intended for the German ambassador in Mexico. This infamous "Zimmerman telegram" instructed the German embassy to approach the Mexican government with an offer of military alliance. The message assumed that the United States ultimately would enter the war and offered Mexico territory in the American southwest if the Germans were victorious in Europe. The significance of the disclosure of this telegram was a new fear that the war was now moving into the Western Hemisphere. The United States was not protected by vast oceans, as noninterventionists had argued. In response, the navy began to arm its merchantmen on the high seas.

Another dramatic set of events occurred only a couple of weeks later, when the tsarist government in Russia was overthrown, opening the door for a democratic government in a country ruled by autocrats for hundreds of years. The revolution in Russia had an impact on Wilson's thinking, for now the war pitted the democracies of France and Great Britain, allied with a fledgling democracy in Russia, against the imperial governments of Germany and Austria-Hungary. This was no small matter, as Wilson and like-minded progressives believed that U.S. power should be guided by higher ideals, particularly the promotion of democracy around the world. Perhaps the Great War could be a war to end autocratic government and usher in an era of peace and democracy throughout Europe.

Yet, while such idealism was at work in Wilson's mind, concerns over self-defense moved events toward war. The German navy, now sure that U.S. entry into the war was a foregone conclusion, launched an uncontained assault in the Atlantic. Within days, three U.S. vessels were sunk. Wilson called a special session of Congress on April 2 to issue a declaration of war.

Much to Roosevelt's frustration, he was out of the country in January when this chain of events began. Daniels had sent him on a tour of the Caribbean, particularly to examine the state of things in Haiti. In 1915, the United States had deployed marines to the island nation to stabilize a society turned upside-down by revolution. While visiting Santo Domingo, he received a cable recalling him to Washington. Throughout

February and March, he readied himself and the navy for war. He and Eleanor attended Wilson's war declaration address to Congress, and as he sat in the gallery he had to have mixed feelings—horror that the war had come home but perhaps somewhat vindicated in his views that the United States could not opt out of the conflict.

Roosevelt's plan all along had been that, in the event of war, he would resign from his civilian position and enlist. Cousin Theodore urged him on, writing to him in the days following the war declaration that "You must resign. You must get into uniform at once." For his part, the elder Roosevelt, now in his fifties and blind in one eye, sought one last hurrah by forming a volunteer regiment to take to France—a repeat of his exploits in the Spanish-American War. He was crushed when he realized that Wilson had no intention of allowing it, for the president believed that the war would best be fought with a fully professionalized military force. Franklin, showing once again his common bond with the "bull moose," criticized Wilson's decision.

Roosevelt also would have to accept the fact that he would not be entering the war either. Both Wilson and Daniels believed that Roosevelt was too critical to the Navy Department to lose to a uniform. He sincerely wanted to serve; however, in the end his superiors managed to convince him that he could do more to defeat the Germans in an administrative role than on the battlefield. Roosevelt would spend the war in Washington, not in France.

There was an enormous amount of work to be done, and while Roosevelt would have preferred to involve himself in matters of military strategy, much of his work was in civilian administration. His responsibilities ranged from overseeing wartime risk insurance, to contacts and defense procurement, to labor negotiations and administration. With respect to procurement, the careful attempts at cost-cutting that had guided Roosevelt and Daniels in prior years were pushed aside to achieve speed and efficiency. As a result, he witnessed firsthand the very real fact of war profiteering, as manufacturers could demand higher prices for goods without the fear of being subjected to competitive bidding. He also came to the view that the key to an efficient and productive defense production system was a smooth relationship between government, private industry, and labor. Organized labor, just as businesses, sought to capitalize on a sudden increase in demand by obtaining higher wages. Greater demands by labor leaders, with the threat of walkouts or slowdowns as a bargaining tool, in Roosevelt's mind were as dangerous to the war effort as businessmen trying to gouge the system.

In response to these concerns, Roosevelt strongly supported the creation of a National War Labor Board, which would bring together the separate entities of the Navy Department and the Labor Department. Although some labor leaders complained that such coordination resulted in less autonomy for workers, Roosevelt came away from the experience convinced of the effectiveness of coordinated planning between labor and the government. In later years as president, both during the Great Depression and World War II, he drew from his experiences as a war administrator to guide policy.

Roosevelt's contributions to defense strategy were limited but noteworthy. Concerned about the dangers of German U-boats attacking the U.S. coastline, he pushed for the creation and deployment of a vast fleet of small, motor-powered boats to patrol the eastern seaboard. There was considerable opposition to the plan due to its costs and questions as to its potential for success. President Wilson doubted seriously whether such small boats, which at one point he referred to as "junk," had any chance of deterring the Germans. Yet Roosevelt was adamant, entering into heated debates with naval officers who disagreed with the need for the deployment. In the end, he won approval of a limited fleet.

A more significant contribution to the war effort, and one that Roosevelt would always claim was his idea alone, was the creation of a mine network in the North Sea to thwart the advances of German submarines. Here he had more support within the navy and the administration but found opposition in England, where the British Admiralty rejected the idea as impractical. Once again, however, Roosevelt would not be denied, and he lobbied energetically for the project with British officials. In the end he prevailed, as the United States Navy funded a line of mines and nets extending from the coast of Scotland across to Norway. By the end of the war, over 70,000 mines had been laid, and, while the mine barrage was not decisive in defeating the Germans, it did destroy several U-boats. In later years, when reminiscing about the war, Roosevelt usually described these defense matters, despite the fact that his primary contributions to the war were in administration.

The war not only changed Roosevelt's life; it also shook up life in the household. Eleanor had spent most of her adult life focused on raising the children and taking care of Franklin. Now, in the midst of a national emergency, she became active in public life in a substantial way for the first time. She volunteered to oversee knitting at the Navy Department's workroom; she also devoted a great deal of time to the Red Cross, preparing food for troops in Washington who were waiting to be deployed to

Europe. She found the work meaningful and became a respected figure among those with whom she worked. The Red Cross even extended her an invitation to travel to England to establish a food program there, which she declined. The war years were pivotal for Eleanor, for she would continue to participate in public causes for the remainder of her life. There was one major drawback, and that was the lack of time she was able to spend with the family, particularly her husband.

While Roosevelt's work was important and often exhausting, throughout the war he continued to feel as though he was playing a backstage role. More than anything, he wanted to travel to Europe—to be closer to the real action and to witness the war for himself. He eventually managed to convince Daniels that it was in the best interest of the navy for one of them to travel there to assess the war's progress. In July 1918, Roosevelt found himself aboard a destroyer, the U.S.S. *Dyer*, headed for Europe. Of all his wartime experiences, he would remember the trip as the highlight of the period and as among the more memorable experiences of his life, despite the fact that little of significance occurred.

Perhaps the trip made such an impact on Roosevelt because, for the first time in his life, and perhaps the only time, he felt part of the military (despite the fact that he would someday be commander-in-chief of all armed forces). He slept in the commander's quarters of the *Dyer*, a new ship that had been commissioned under Roosevelt's watch. He fraternized with the officers on board and spoke often with enlisted men. He wrote about the trip in considerable detail in a journal. One of his favorite stories from the journey, and one that he would retell for years to come, had to do with a German U-boat that passed some fifty miles from the ship. One biographer has noted that in later years, the more the story was told, the submarine came closer and closer, to the point that it passed right beside the ship.

Following a brief stay in England, during which he discussed matters of strategy with members of the British command, Roosevelt landed at Dunkirk and moved inland to see the front lines firsthand. His party traveled through Boulogne and Abbeville toward Paris, where he stayed at the luxurious Hotel Crillon as an official guest of the government. While in the city, he met the president, Raymond Poincare, and the French premier, Georges Clemenceau. Roosevelt then traveled on to Bellau Wood, where he finally witnessed combat, as a U.S. gun battery was firing on a German position several miles away. The scene was dramatic—while the thunder of the battery echoed through the forest, overhead German and Allied planes were locked in a firefight, scenes that Roosevelt wrote about in detail in his journal. Later he moved on to visit Chateau Thierry, Nancy, and Verdun.

In later years, much was made of his tour to the battlefields of France, both by Roosevelt himself and his critics. In 1936, commenting on the deteriorating situation in Europe once again, he explained solemnly in a speech that he "had seen war." Such words met with derision from those who believed Roosevelt was trying to portray himself as an active participant in the war for political effect. Certainly Roosevelt did not experience war as had so many thousands of enlisted men, but he did see the devastation caused by the war. He visited field hospitals, witnessed the stench of the trenches, spoke with exhausted and often bewildered soldiers, and saw the destruction of the natural environment. The extent to which the experience altered his views of war is impossible to say. Other than his journal entries of the time, which offer little more than a chronological account of the trip, he neither wrote nor spoke a great deal about it in later years. In fact, the speech given almost 15 years later was one of the few times that he acknowledged the journey.

The return home was harrowing, as he contracted a serious case of pneumonia compounded by influenza; he was so ill that he had to be carried off the ship on a stretcher when he arrived in New York. Bedridden for almost a month, he was unable to work during the last stages of the war. By the time Roosevelt was on his feet again, the war was only weeks from ending. He even entertained the notion of enlisting in October in order to have a chance to serve before the fighting was over. Yet he did not; there would be plenty of work in the Navy Department even following the armistice.

His bout with illness was only one crisis he faced that autumn. The other had a much more lasting impact—the discovery by Eleanor that Franklin had been involved in a romantic relationship with her social secretary, Lucy Mercer. While Franklin was convalescing, Eleanor evidently came across letters Mercer had written to her husband that had been stashed away in his papers. Mercer had worked for the Roosevelt family since 1913 and was almost the opposite of Eleanor—young, vivacious and extroverted, and very attractive. When the relationship began was unclear; more than likely it started the year before Franklin left for Europe. Eleanor was devastated and, according to some accounts, contemplated ending the marriage. She would come away from the experience a changed woman.

She perhaps had suspected that something of this nature was taking place months earlier. Eleanor could accept the fact that her husband was outgoing, and at times even flirtatious. There had been times in the past where both had commented on Roosevelt's charm—usually in a joking manner. Yet the demands of his job had pulled them apart, and they were seldom together. Mercer often accompanied Franklin on business outings, and her name increasingly showed up in his letters in 1917. Yet while he may have been taken by the pretty Mercer, he also continued to display strong affection for his family, including Eleanor. Whether the relationship was anything more than a fling is unclear. According to one account, Franklin contemplated leaving the family to marry Lucy but discovered that she would not be willing to go along with such a plan.

Details of the entire affair always have been sketchy. Roosevelt himself never mentioned it, and Eleanor remained silent until much later, choosing to discuss the matter only much later in life, and particularly after Franklin died. Clearly Eleanor was stung sharply by the news and went into a period of deep despair. The historian Joseph Lash, who interviewed Eleanor extensively during her final years, claimed that the couple seriously contemplated divorce but that pressure from Sara Roosevelt, and the realization that Franklin's career would be ruined by such a scandal, prevented the break from occurring.

While these private details may never be verifiable, it is certain that following the incident their relationship changed permanently. Never again would their marriage be marked by the warm and romantic affection of their younger years. She would stay with Franklin and continue to support his career; however, she also became much more independent. In a letter she wrote to Lash decades later, she recounted her feelings at the time without mentioning the affair explicitly. "The bottom dropped out of my world and I faced myself, my surroundings, my world, honestly for the first time. I really grew up that year." Their relationship was complicated. They were friends, partners, and companions; clearly Eleanor continued to love him in some ways. However, their lives became much more separate after the ordeal.

Only weeks after these troubles, the armistice was announced ending the war. Wilson immediately began to make plans to travel to Paris to participate in the settlement with other Allied leaders. Roosevelt desperately wanted to go and was unfazed when Daniels answered an initial inquiry with a denial. After following up his initial request with a pleading letters, his boss relented. Everyone knew that the deliberations in Paris would be among the most historic events in recent history, perhaps in all of world history. Although Roosevelt would not attend the conferences as an official member of the president's team, Daniels did offer him instructions to participate in negotiations regarding demobilization of U.S. troops in France. On January 1, 1919, he and Eleanor embarked for Europe.

The trip was unremarkable, and Roosevelt's work was somewhat mundane, but he was satisfied in being a part of these memorable events. For the return home, he and Eleanor sailed on the same ship with Wilson, and all arrived in Boston greeted by an uproarious crowd of over 200,000 onlookers. The mood among Wilson's staff was triumphant, as the president had managed to achieve his primary goal of creating a League of Nations covenant that was approved by the membership of the treaties. The formation of the League had become Wilson's passion in the final months of the war, for he believed that a congress of nation-states could help to avoid the senseless rivalries responsible for the conflict. While the treaty would have to be ratified by a two-thirds majority in the Senate, the administration was confident that the United States would join, thus truly making World War I a "war to end all wars."

Roosevelt returned to Washington to carry out his duties in the Navy Department for the remainder of Wilson's term. While he naturally had begun to consider his future, his final year in the position proved to be among the more difficult. First, there was the League of Nations issue. Although the administration had been confident early on that the Senate would approve the treaty, U.S. entry into the international organization came under fire by most Republicans and even some Democrats. Throughout the spring and summer of 1919, Wilson engaged in heated public debate with his opponents, particularly the Republican Senator Henry Cabot Lodge, who not only spoke forcefully against the treaty but also lined up opposition in Congress to defeat the measure. By August, the treaty was languishing on the Senate floor; it was becoming more and more apparent that the United States would not join. Wilson responded by taking a whirlwind tour across the nation speaking in favor of the League. Already in poor health, the trip exhausted him, and in October he collapsed from a stroke while traveling in the West. He returned to Washington a near invalid; for the remainder of his presidency Wilson was unable to work without the close supervision of his wife and doctors.

While Wilson's political and physical failures were concerns for everyone in the administration, Roosevelt faced his own share of problems. For one, the end of the war meant a sharp decline in government demand for manufactures, a change that would impact workers directly as wages would begin to decline and layoffs would inevitably occur. A first sign of trouble appeared when a strike of tugboat workers in New York threatened to cut off coal supplies for the entire city. By the summer of 1919, strikes were exploding in a variety of industries; ultimately more labor walkouts and pickets occurred that year than any year in U.S. history. As Roosevelt had been in charge of civilian labor during the war, he was expected to help smooth the transition back to a peacetime economy. Furthermore, he understood the political importance of labor; pondering his own political future, he feared taking sides with corporate leaders. In most cases, he attempted to chart a moderate course. He became even more committed to the idea that labor-management conflict could be ameliorated through government action. At a minimum, this could be achieved through piecemeal arbitration. Ideally, the government would establish a permanent labor relations board modeled after the National War Labor Board. The experience would shape his later policies with respect to the labor movement.

Other crises began to surface. In the spring of 1920, Roosevelt made a terrible decision to back an oil refining scheme designed by a group of speculators, some of them personal friends. Due to decreasing supplies and an explosion in demand during wartime, the price of oil had skyrocketed—a trend that seemed to benefit the larger oil companies. Roosevelt, before the war, had prided himself on the job that the Navy Department had done to confront cartels and monopolies and thus lower costs. The idea here was to purchase Mexican crude, which had historically been viewed as of such poor quality as to be unusable, and to transport it using navy ships to Massachusetts, where a new company, the New England Oil Corporation, would refine it and sell it to the navy at a price lower than the current market rate, thus saving the government money.

There were several murky details about the deal beyond the fact that several of the investors had close ties to Roosevelt. New England Oil's headquarters were to be constructed in Louis Howe's wife's hometown. Such a setup would have been plenty of political fodder for opponents. However, to make matters worse, as the new company was refining its first petroleum, a spike in supply sharply lowered oil prices. Suddenly, the navy was paying more for the oil produced by this hastily constructed company than on the open market. While Roosevelt was never found to be guilty of illegal activities, the entire affair was one of poor judgment.

To add to this mounting mess, by the spring of 1920 the Senate Naval Affairs Committee had launched investigations into alleged mismanagement in the Navy Department during the war. Ironically, Roosevelt may have played a part in triggering these actions, for throughout the war he had made a habit of complaining to officers about the lack of effective leadership from Daniels. Now, to Roosevelt's horror, one of those commanders, Admiral William S. Sims, began to publicize charges of inefficiency in the department. While Roosevelt may have had his quibbles with Daniels, he had no desire to see the navy raked over the coals, which would also be an indictment of his own leadership abilities.

Republicans in the Congress smelled blood—because these accusations were being made in an election year, they could perhaps cast the Democratic administration in a poor light. As the Senate launched its investigations, accusations of problems within the navy moved into other areas. Among the most publicized was the claim that vice and corruption had become rampant in the naval prison system. There were more ironies. Daniels and Roosevelt, when first entering their positions in the department, had made a commitment to reform navy prisons. Within the past year, Roosevelt also had approved the creation of investigative squads that would look for evidence of immoral behavior in the prisons. Now, however, accusations were emerging that many members of these so-called squads had been guilty of immoral acts themselves. Roosevelt appeared before the committee on multiple occasions to defend his own actions and the actions of Daniels.

By this time, Roosevelt was ready to leave his position in the navy. On the whole, he performed well in the job although he had made some errors of judgment. If at times he was guilty of overzealousness, petty jealousy, and ambition, he also took his job very seriously and believed that he was playing a role in making the United States Navy the best in the world. Perhaps most importantly, despite several difficult challenges, Roosevelt managed to survive his first years in Washington without damaging his name beyond repair. In most circles, he was considered a rising star in U.S. politics. Over the next few years, his star did rise, but only in the face of extraordinary hurdles.

Chapter 5

DEFEAT AND TRAGEDY

In 1919, while Roosevelt was finishing up his duties in the Navy Department, the question loomed as to whether he would continue in politics or take time off from public life. Eleanor was clear in her preference for Franklin to take a vacation from politics. Now with five children, she sought some stability for the family. There also were financial considerations. While the Roosevelts were comfortable and always might count on the support of Franklin's mother Sara, his salary in Washington had been lower than that to which they were accustomed. What made sense to her was a return to business for a few years. Certainly Roosevelt would be a strong candidate for a number of possibilities on Wall Street, given his vast contacts in both New York and Washington. During his final years in government, in fact, he had begun to make inquiries into possible private employment.

Yet the pull of politics was strong. Newspapers across the country already had begun to mention Roosevelt as a leading figure in the party. In New York, a few articles had appeared that offered his name as a candidate for the upcoming United States Senate election. One suggested that Roosevelt could become the next governor of the state. And some editorials, even outside New York, opened up the possibility that he might be presidential material.

Having now been in government for almost a decade, he was realistic regarding where he stood in his party. The presidency was not, in his mind, a viable option. While he had a strong base of support in some parts of his home state, he was aware that the path to the White House required the careful assembling of a national organization within the party. Furthermore, he believed, along with many other people, that the political winds were shifting and that public support for "Wilsonianism" was on the decline. Most political prognosticators viewed 1920 as a year for the Republicans. If Roosevelt was serious about becoming the president, and evidently by this time he had begun to at least consider the prospect, the timing would have to be right.

That left the New York races—either for the governorship or the U.S. Senate. While either of these offices clearly would be considered a step up the political ladder, neither would be an easy win, even for the nomination of his own party. The incumbent governor was Democrat Al Smith, a party veteran with statewide popularity and a man in good standing with his party. Roosevelt respected Smith and had supported him in earlier elections. Should he decide to run for reelection, there was little hope that party leaders would be interested in changing candidates. However, there were rumors that Smith had some interest in running for the open Senate seat, which would give Roosevelt a chance at the nomination for governor. These scenarios would have to be sorted out at the 1920 Democratic party convention, which was held in San Francisco. Here the New York delegates would select their nominee for the Senate seat and clear up Roosevelt's future plans.

One strong indication that Roosevelt's mind was already made up regarding his political future was his decision to attend the convention. Eleanor probably by this time had accepted the fact that her husband had no intention of leaving politics right away and stood by to hear how things developed out west. Early on at the convention, which began in late June, Smith announced his desire to be reelected as governor. Roosevelt's name soon was brought forward with a handful of others as candidates for the Senate nomination. Yet following a few days of deliberation, it became clear that the nomination would most likely go to someone else. Part of the reason may have been Roosevelt's decision to challenge Tammany on voting procedure, which irritated Charles Murphy. Furthermore, Roosevelt had gone out of his way to honor President Wilson on the floor of the convention, which ran counter to the attitudes of the machine, which never supported him enthusiastically.

Roosevelt's skirmishes with Tammany at the convention, however, were not that significant. In fact, relations between Murphy and Roosevelt had warmed during the war years. The main factor in determining Roosevelt's fate at the convention may have been Roosevelt himself, who did not actively plug for the nomination. He may have been of the mind that, given the state of politics in New York, any Democratic nominee would face an uphill battle in the general election. For a time it seemed that he would come away from the convention empty-handed.

Yet even as these developments were unfolding, Roosevelt's name began circulating as a potential running mate for whoever won the nomination for president. Such a scenario was not unexpected, because his name had appeared in the press on several occasions regarding such a role. However, in the months leading up the convention he had rejected such talk as unrealistic, perhaps because he had focused his attention on the New York elections. Now, however, the possibilities seemed great, a fact that he indicated in his letters to Eleanor.

Roosevelt's selection as the vice presidential candidate on the ticket depended a great deal on who would win the presidential nomination. The process was delicate, for he could not put his own name forward but had to wait for events to unfold around him. The front-runner at the beginning of the convention was William Gibbs McAdoo, who had served as secretary of the treasury under Wilson. He was attractive particularly to the party's southern base, not only because he was a Wilson man but also because he was a strong supporter of Prohibition. The Eighteenth Amendment to the Constitution, which made the sale of alcohol illegal, had been ratified the year before; nevertheless, Prohibition remained an important issue and was considered by many people to be the central issue of the election. Also running was A. Mitchell Palmer, who had made a name for himself as Wilson's attorney general by carrying out infamous raids against suspected radicals during the past year.

If either of these candidates were to win the nomination, Roosevelt knew that his chances of being selected as a running mate were slim. Both were Wilson men, and the Democratic party would most likely want to add an "outsider" to the ticket to placate voters who were critical of the president. Although Roosevelt at times had his differences with the administration, particularly over issues of defense policy, he was still a stalwart supporter of his boss and defended his record at those times in the convention when anti-Wilson voices made their presence known. Being a supporter of the president was an asset at the convention for obvious reasons, as the Democrats had devoted eight years to championing the former Princetonian. However, there was a large contingent of delegates who did not support Wilson, particularly in the isolationist-minded Midwest and among machine politicians in the eastern cities, particularly New York.

The final candidate who had serious backing was Ohio Governor James Cox, an attractive figure to many delegates because of his middle-of-the-road status in the party. While he openly supported the United States' entry into the League of Nations, he had not been a part of the administration. He also positioned himself as a moderate on the alcohol issue. Cox also was from a swing state, the same state of the Republican nominee, Warren G. Harding. He also was a good match for Roosevelt, and party insiders agreed that Roosevelt would be the clear front-runner for the ticket if Cox won.

The convention quickly deadlocked, and for several days it was unclear which of these men would emerge victorious. Roosevelt maintained a low profile during the voting, for he had established himself as a loyal Wilsonian but understood the ramifications of a victory for McAdoo or Palmer. Finally, late in the evening of July 4, delegates began to break for Cox. On the forty-third ballot, the Ohioan won. By the following midday, it was clear that Roosevelt would be offered the vice presidential slot. When his name was announced on the floor to shouts of "Roosevelt, Roosevelt, We Want Roosevelt," he made sure to be out of the convention hall to avoid appearing to want the position. In typical political fashion of the times, he feigned complete surprise when the decision was announced, despite the fact that he had known the probable outcome since the night before.

Considering Roosevelt's keen sense of political timing, his acceptance of the nomination could be questioned. Most people, even Democrats, expected that Warren G. Harding, the newspaper man from Marion, Ohio, along with running mate Calvin Coolidge of Vermont, would win the election. The reasons for such predictions were several. For one, the past year had been a very troubled one for the administration, as the nation faced an economic slump, labor upheaval, race riots in cities, and a scare over radical subversion. The Democratic party was also badly divided between its progressive, reformist wing and its more conservative southern wing. Roosevelt understood all of this, making several private comments at the time that the campaign would most likely be a losing cause. He also was aware, however, that serving as a running mate was not the same as running at the top of the ticket. This was Cox's race, and even if they lost the election, Roosevelt would have enjoyed yet another opportunity to appear on the national stage while avoiding the label of loser.

Despite such dire forecasts, Roosevelt plunged into the campaign with his typical enthusiasm. He looked forward to traveling the campaign trail, speaking on the stump, and debating with his opponents. In his acceptance speech, which he gave at Hyde Park, he pledged to support an active foreign policy and declared that the United States could ill-afford to retreat into what he referred to as pre–World War I isolationism—a clear endorsement of the League of Nations Charter. He also echoed the party platform of making government more efficient, particularly by applying business principles to the running of government bureaucracies. In what became a regular campaign message, Roosevelt also played up his youth and attempted to portray the Democratic ticket as one of energy and forward thinking.

While domestic issues had their place in the campaign, the contest seemed to be centered on foreign policy; both parties in fact considered the election to be a referendum on Wilson's League of Nations. Roosevelt sincerely believed that if Americans were educated on the true nature of the organization they would come to see its importance. In speech after speech, he spoke passionately for ratification of the treaty. He also proved to be adept at tailoring his messages to fit particular audiences. In urban areas, particularly when speaking before groups that contained larger numbers of professional-oriented middle-class voters, the League Covenant was the major theme. In rural areas where the majority of onlookers were farmers, his words took a populist tone, as he railed against special interests such as big business and political bosses.

The campaign turned out to be exhausting. In August alone Roosevelt traveled to more than 20 states, and on one occasion he gave 26 speeches within 48 hours. Despite its grueling nature, he truly enjoyed the experience, indicated by cheerful letters he wrote to Eleanor describing developments on the trail. In line with her own lack of fondness for campaigning and public attention generally, Eleanor stayed at Campobello and awaited word on Franklin's whereabouts.

In September, Roosevelt sent word to Eleanor that he would like for her to join him on the campaign. This was not something to which she had looked forward. Early in the campaign, in fact, she had refused to offer the campaign a photograph for use in the press, forcing newspapers to search for any pictures of the couple that had been published earlier. The culture of campaign also was not appealing—the constant traveling, eating at odd hours, mingling with the almost completely male entourage. She agreed to join him as requested but found the experience somewhat lonely and altogether tiring. Often Franklin would stay up late with "the boys," playing poker and smoking cigars following a day's events. Eleanor usually retired early and considered the trip an ordeal.

Overall, Roosevelt ran a strong campaign for Cox. He effectively promoted the League Covenant, expecting this issue would offer voters a clear choice. He did make one serious gaffe during the campaign while speaking in Montana. During a heated discussion over the details of the

League, in which critics complained that Great Britain would have inordinate influence in the organization due to its multiple votes, Roosevelt made statements that created a stir in the press. First, he pointed out that the United States was firmly in control of the Western Hemisphere, implying that the nations of Latin America, having votes in the League of Nations, would in effect be controlled by the position of the United States. Republican critics derided Roosevelt's "blatant imperialism" and lack of respect for the sovereignty of nations south of the border. But he did not leave the issue there; Roosevelt also explained that he had himself written Haiti's constitution, which illustrated the degree to which the United States had influence in the Americas. The claim also was absolutely false. Roosevelt had, of course, visited Haiti while working in the Navy Department and had played a role in the formation of U.S. policy toward that country. However, his assertion regarding the constitution made little sense and might best be explained as typical Roosevelt bravado. The press, and particularly newspaper editorialists who supported Harding, played up the mistake.

In the end, however, Roosevelt's disaster in Montana had little effect on the election's outcome and quickly disappeared from the public eye. As the campaign came to a close, most newspapers continued to predict a Republican victory. Roosevelt no doubt expected this outcome, even though in a few letters written in the final weeks of campaigning he hinted that the Democrats might pull off a surprise. He and Eleanor returned home to Hyde Park in early November to await the results, and as the news trickled in it became apparent that the news was not good. What was most troubling was not the fact that the ticket had fallen short, but rather the margin of victory. Harding and Coolidge won more than 60 percent of the popular vote, and the Electoral College tally was 404 to 127, the most lopsided election in a hundred years.

Typically, though, Roosevelt received the news in good spirits. No one near him recalled that after the election he displayed any disappointment at all. Sara, in fact, wrote at the time that he seemed to be "relieved not to be elected Vice-President." He immediately wired Calvin Coolidge, the vice-president-elect, with a message of congratulations. With time he became somewhat philosophical about the election, coming to believe that America's turn to a conservative voice was inevitable given the considerable tumult of the war years. If anything, the experience may have reinforced the lesson regarding politics that he already had come to realize—that timing always was crucial. There would be more, and no doubt better, opportunities with time.

For the first time in a decade, Roosevelt was out of government and would have some time to ponder his future. He also was unemployed, and his first impulse was to follow up on his precampaign plans of entering the corporate world and bringing some stability back into his life and that of the family—plans that Eleanor no doubt greeted warmly. Finding a position in the private sector would not be a daunting task given Roosevelt's vast contacts in both government and business. He decided to take a position with the New York branch of the Fidelity and Deposit Company of Maryland, a large bonding firm that underwrote corporations. As an attorney for the company, he garnered a comfortable but not extravagant salary of $25,000. Now back on Wall Street, he would have the opportunity to reenter the social world there that he had enjoyed briefly before moving into the state legislature years earlier.

Life for the family may have calmed down somewhat but certainly was not less busy. Eleanor, while happy to see campaigning out of the picture at least for a while, nevertheless had no intentions of returning to her earlier roles of mother and wife. Determined to be more independent, she plunged into several activities. Some were attempts to establish her new-found sense of autonomy, such as learning to cook and to drive a car. She also spent less time working for Franklin and more time working for her own causes. She agreed to join the board of the League of Women Voters, where she found meaningful work and made several lasting professional relationships. In January 1921 she attended the League's state convention as a delegate from Hyde Park. Soon she had become an icon in the organization.

Franklin's own schedule quickly filled up. He decided that in addition to his work with Fidelity and Deposit, he also would begin a new law partnership. Each day he spent mornings working for his primary employer and afternoons working in his law office. He also began to take on a large number of positions in charity and volunteer organizations, including the Overseers of Harvard University, the Navy Club, and the New York Committee of the Boy Scouts of America. If these commitments were not enough, in the summer of 1921 he was forced to travel to Washington to testify before the Senate Naval Affairs Committee, whose investigation into the Wilson administration's handling of the navy continued. By the end of the summer, this frenetic pace began to wear on him. He began to complain of fatigue.

By early August, he was back at Campobello, spending his days sailing and fishing in an attempt at rejuvenation. On August 10, following a day of sailing and exploring, he returned home feeling quite weak. He plunged into the cold waters of Fundy Bay to refresh himself, had dinner, and went to bed early. He awoke the next morning to find that his legs were so weak that he could barely stand. The following morning the condition was worse, and within a few hours he could not stand at all. He also began to experience a fever.

Locating a doctor in such a remote setting was not easy. An elderly doctor from Philadelphia who was vacationing nearby visited him on August 13 and determined that the problem was temporary paralysis, probably brought on by a blood clot in his spinal cord. He advised continual back and leg massages to relieve the clot, and for a few days Eleanor and Louis Howe, who was visiting, alternated giving him vigorous rubdowns. Soon the decision was made to bring in a professional masseuse to carry out the therapy regularly.

Days passed without improvement and everyone began to suspect that the problem was worse than first assumed. Two weeks after the initial attack, a Boston doctor was brought in who diagnosed infantile paralysis, otherwise known as poliomyelitis. The doctor softened the blow by assuring Roosevelt that the case was mild and that he should be back on his feet in a matter of weeks. In September, Roosevelt traveled to New York by train to be treated by specialists. By now the news had reached the public, and Roosevelt noted, while boarding the train for the city, a small crowd of supporters and reporters at the station. This bothered him, because he had every intention of keeping the illness a secret.

Roosevelt dispatched Howe to assure the press that the condition would be short-lived. Doctors, however, were beginning to conclude that the muscles in his legs and back were damaged to the point that walking, and perhaps even sitting upright, would be impossible. However, no one knew for sure the extent of the damage, and over the next couple of weeks his condition improved a bit, as the muscles in his back strengthened to the point that he could once again sit upright. If this sort of improvement continued, then all would be well. "The doctors," Roosevelt wrote in a letter in early December, "say there is no question that by Spring I will be walking without a limp."

The winter months were excruciating. Not only had he lost the use of both legs, but now he faced intense pain almost constantly. With what can only be described as gritty determination, he tried to work through the pain and strengthen his muscles. He began wearing steel braces that ran the entire length of his legs; with time he learned to stand on them and even move a bit by using his hips to pivot his weight. In all, there was little progress, and it became more and more clear that the damage was permanent.

This realization meant new changes for the entire household. Roosevelt's condition placed a strain on the family, as each member later recalled these hard times. Eleanor at this time was remarkable. She tended to her husband around the clock and continued to watch over the children. Sara early on was not much help to her. The matron of the family now alternated between moods of wanting to play a more active role in helping her son and bitterness, and even some pettiness, when she felt unable to control things. She also resented the fact that Louis Howe was closer to Franklin than she was, as he had moved into the house permanently to help. Sara never liked him, once referring to him as "that dirty little man," and even tried to drive a wedge between Eleanor and Franklin's daughter Anna and her mother by claiming that Howe was more favored in the household than the children. With time the relationship between Howe, Sara, and the rest of the family improved, particularly as they realized the extreme level of devotion Howe had for his boss.

If Eleanor's life had been transformed during the war years, more changes came during these dark days. If she had deferred decisions to Franklin and Sara in years past, now, with her husband bedridden, she took control of the entire household. Perhaps most notable was her decision to do everything in her power to see Franklin's career continue. This ran counter to Sara's wishes; she tried to convince her son that his disability was a sign that he should resign from public life and move back to Hyde Park to live a life of relaxation. Eleanor knew her husband, however, perhaps better than Sara, and understood that Franklin could not live the life-style of the country squire with any sense of fulfillment. Besides, he seemed determined to overcome the setback and carry on with his work. She admired him for that and committed herself to the same goal.

There would, of course, be changes. Although Roosevelt would eventually come to accept the presence of wheelchairs, braces, and crutches to aid in mobility, he would never be able to zip from place to place as he had before. Roosevelt also had to concede that he would be less independent now and had to rely on those around him. Eleanor, Howe, and new personal secretary Marguerite (Missy) LeHand became part of a team, with Franklin serving as its captain. The four of them began to plan activities that would assure the public that he was not withdrawing from the world permanently. Each of them handled the press at times, and each of them played a part in determining Roosevelt's next moves. Early on the team examined his various volunteer responsibilities and determined which ones would have to be eliminated. Some, such as the Navy Club, were jettisoned. Others, such as his work with the Boy Scouts of America, an organization for which Roosevelt had much passion, remained.

All things considered, Roosevelt's activities during his first year or so of having polio were impressive. He continued as an active player in politics, business, and charity work. His role in the Democratic party of New York diminished little. While he did not make nearly as many public appearances, he worked at home to influence the course of events, such as playing a significant role in supporting Al Smith in the 1922 governor's race and helping him to secure the party's nomination. By this time, discussion of Roosevelt again running for office was in full force, if it ever had subsided at all.

Part of the reason for this continuity in his career lay in the fact that he and the "team" worked energetically to keep his disability from public view. Certainly people were aware of his condition, but Roosevelt was committed to making sure that it was not something with which he would be identified. He perfected strategies to mask his lack of mobility. He avoided being photographed in a wheelchair or with crutches and learned how he could even seem to be walking by locking arms with one of his aids. These efforts yielded impressive results, for many Americans never fully realized the extent of his disability, even after he became president. Critics, then and now, might explain this behavior as an example of Roosevelt being the consummate politician, for he feared that displaying his disability could be perceived by the public as a sign of weakness. Undoubtedly the political impact of his condition was a consideration. However, another factor here was pride, for Roosevelt seemed to hate the idea that he would be defined by physical impairment—not only in the public eye but also within his own family and social circle.

Eleanor's transformation went deeper than taking on more of a role in Roosevelt's career. In surprising ways, the tragedy led her to become much more independent. She took on several new responsibilities, some of them related to her husband's political career and others rooted in her own interests and ambitions. She took an active role in organizing women in the Democratic party across the state, which brought her into contact with the entire party organization as it began to see the very real dividends that grassroots organizing could have for all candidates. She overcame her reluctance to speak in public; with the help of both Howe and Franklin, she sharpened her skills as an orator and as a political strategist. Letters she wrote during this time indicated that her knowledge of political issues and political process increased by leaps and bounds—a remarkable change for a woman who only a few years earlier had refused to even be photographed.

Biographers of Roosevelt have addressed the impact of polio on his career as well as his personality. Many observers believe that these were pivotal years, and some have concluded that his physical impairment actually turned out to be an asset. According to this line of thinking, Roosevelt was an able politician in his earlier years but was hampered by his enthusiasm. At times, where caution or careful calculation might have served him well, his temper got the best of him. Some who knew him in those days described him as somewhat flighty, given to acting on impulse, and unable to think through problems with maturity. His illness brought him down to earth, so the argument went, making him more thoughtful and more stable. If there was something of the playboy in the younger Roosevelt, that personality had given way to a man with clearer vision and deeper thinking. In fact, some biographers have suggested that his bout with polio was the decisive moment in his life, and that without it he probably would have never reached the political heights that he did.

Others have suggested that Roosevelt's illness was yet another sign of his gift of political timing. The thinking here is that the 1920s was a time of retreat for the Democratic party everywhere in the country; had Roosevelt continued to run for office during this time, he most certainly would have suffered defeat. The party was also polarized to the point that he would be forced to alienate large blocs of voters, making any attempts at national campaigning much more difficult. His temporary withdrawal from public office, as the argument went, allowed him to weather this storm, and by the late 1920s, as the Democrats began to recover, Roosevelt was perfectly positioned by virtue of not carrying any political baggage from those years.

These perspectives on Roosevelt's illness have some elements of truth. Even people quite close to him remarked on a change of personality brought on by the ordeal. Some who considered him arrogant, for example, recalled that his demeanor took on a much more warm and likeable countenance in the years after polio. As for politics, the decade certainly was a time of Republican ascendancy, as the party held onto the White House for the entirety of the Roaring Twenties. At the same time, legends of the illness somehow remaking Roosevelt also are a bit exaggerated. His political views changed little during these years, and his respite from political life lasted only months rather than years. For much of the public, particularly outside New York, Roosevelt had never actually left public life.

Regardless of the long-term effects of polio, his ability to overcome such a physical, as well as emotional, setback stands as an admirable achievement. Within a year, he had gained back much of his energy and drive and looked forward to returning to business and politics. Now with the "team" around him and with Eleanor fully committed to helping with a comeback, Roosevelt returned to the public stage. Whether he knew it or not, his career was far from reaching its zenith.

Chapter 6

THE RETURN

By the fall of 1922, only about a year after the diagnosis of infantile paralysis, Roosevelt had returned to his position with Fidelity and Deposit on Wall Street. Eventually he was back to a fairly normal schedule, working four days a week. Soon after that, his schedule once again became quite full. He returned to his law firm, began serving again on the boards of some charitable organizations, and still devoted a great deal of time to politics. Louis Howe continued to work around the clock as an all-encompassing political advisor, while Missy LeHand took on increasing responsibilities in the Roosevelt "enterprise." With Eleanor offering her own support, Roosevelt was ready to attempt a comeback.

Despite the fact that his physical condition had not improved much at all, he continued to hold out hope for a recovery. He consulted with an array of specialists searching for new treatments. In the meantime, he worked daily to build strength in his arms and upper body, which he would have to rely on for movement. Eventually he was able to hold himself erect on his braces and even have limited mobility, using his arms to carry his entire weight. All of this work began to change his appearance as he became stockier above the waist.

More than one doctor had suggested to Roosevelt that he spend as much time as possible in warm water as a means of therapy. As a treatment, the suggestion was questionable, but there was no doubt that swimming was good exercise. It also was good mental therapy, as the feeling of weightlessness while swimming allowed him to "walk" more normally. For the remainder of his life, he spent as much time as possible in the water.

This search for therapeutic waters led Roosevelt to acquire a resort property located in Warm Springs, Georgia. The property, owned by businessman George Foster Peabody, had been a prosperous vacation spot in the nineteenth century, as wealthier Americans flocked there to enjoy the warm natural springs that crisscrossed the scenic landscape. Now quite rundown and badly in need of renovation, Peabody was more than willing to let it go. Roosevelt, on the tip of a friend, visited in the summer of 1924 and immediately wanted to make it a regular destination. For weeks he stayed there, swimming in the spring-fed waters and soaking up sunshine.

The resort also received rejuvenation. Newspaper reporters covering Roosevelt's visits generated free publicity, and soon other victims of polio were inquiring about the possibilities of giving the warm waters there a try. Within a couple of years the property was becoming something of a clinic, which prompted Roosevelt to consider the idea of turning it into a modern treatment facility. After purchasing the resort, he formed the Warm Springs Foundation to raise funds for a complete renovation and began soliciting a variety of potential donors. Ultimately, Warm Springs became a highly regarded polio treatment center with a worldwide reputation. Roosevelt also made it a home away from home. Gradually the Georgia location replaced Campobello as his preferred place for relaxation.

The purchase of Warm Springs may have lifted his spirits, but it also placed financial strains on the family, as Sara refused to help finance the project. He had stretched simply to buy the property; there was no way he could afford the construction and renovation plans he envisioned with his income from Wall Street. Back home, money was never tight, but Roosevelt must have felt a bit of pressure to generate more financial security for the family. As a result, he began to spend some of his time searching for investment opportunities to supplement the family income.

His myriad investments and ventures yielded few impressive results. While he was gifted in the world of politics, his business acumen left something to be desired—a quality perhaps inherited from his father. In fact, his business activities in some ways were quite similar to those of James Roosevelt decades earlier. Some of these ventures were a bit outlandish, such as an investment in a company that planned to build dirigibles with passenger service between major U.S. cities. He dabbled in a scheme to import herbal tea from Argentina. He considered developing a chain of resorts along the eastern seaboard modeled after the Warm Springs property. Another venture was a company focused on coin-operated vending machines.

None of these speculations struck gold. Again like his father, Roosevelt seemed to enjoy the excitement of plunging into these ventures and was less interested in developing sound and long-term business plans. He also resembled James in knowing in the back of his mind that these activities were not of extreme importance. The family fortune offered long-range financial security, and while at times things seemed a little tighter than Roosevelt would have preferred, he was never in danger of losing the comforts he and Eleanor had lived with for their entire lives. He never risked huge amounts of money in these schemes, and if anything they offered him another outlet—a means of meeting new people and building more professional relationships. There are few indications, for example, that Eleanor was at all concerned about these business experiments.

Roosevelt never retreated from political life during his illness, but in the few years following his polio he was forced into something of a holding pattern. These were dark days for the Democratic party nationally. The 1924 election had been a disaster. Still badly divided, the party ran John W. Davis against the current vice president, Calvin Coolidge. With a strong economy and the Republican party more united, the election was another landslide. Roosevelt, under advisement from Howe, came to the view that the party required serious reorganization, in New York and around the country. Grass-roots organizing in rural, upstate New York had yielded visible dividends for the party; both men sought to encourage the same kind of resurgence in other states. Roosevelt also was certain that the Democrats would have to find some way to heal the wounds created by nasty infighting between its southern, western, and northeastern wings.

The scene in New York may have been a bit rosier than in other places, but certainly the party was not healthy. The cohesion enjoyed during the Wilson years had eroded. Charles Murphy, the infamous but brilliant leader of Tammany, had been forced to leave politics due to age, leaving New York City's machine in the hands of much less experienced leaders. The historic divisions between country and city were reopening, and Howe believed firmly that Roosevelt should avoid running for office at any time in the near future. In 1926, party leaders contacted Roosevelt about running for the United States Senate, an office that only a few years ago he had considered most attractive. At the urging of Howe and Eleanor, he demurred, stating publicly that he needed more time for recuperation.

The governorship, the position that Roosevelt really wanted, was locked up during these years by Al Smith, who in 1926 was elected to a fourth term. This was an acceptable scenario for Franklin, who continued to support Smith and had no doubt reached the conclusion that perhaps the course of action would be to help vault Smith into the White House at some point in the future, thereby offering Roosevelt an opportunity to fill the void in Albany. Over the next year, this plan seemed to be working well, for Smith began to drop hints that he might make a run for the presidency in 1928. Few other high-profile Democrats seemed interested in the nomination, and most party leaders assumed that it would be his to lose.

The 1928 presidential election for the Roosevelt team became the target for new opportunities, but this optimism always was moderated by a dose of realism. The Republican party continued to hold sway over voters. Furthermore, the Roosevelt cause took an even stronger blow when President Coolidge announced his intention to step aside at the end of his term and return to Vermont, which meant that the Republicans would most likely nominate Secretary of Commerce Herbert Hoover. This was not the best of news for Democrats, including Roosevelt. Americans adored Hoover, who had achieved great fame for his humanitarian efforts during World War I as administrator of food relief in war-torn Belgium. He also carried strong progressive credentials but appealed to the business classes for his economic conservatism. Only a few years earlier, in fact, Roosevelt on numerous occasions had remarked that Hoover would be an excellent candidate for the Democratic party.

This turn of events compelled Howe and Roosevelt to rethink their strategy, eventually coming to the conclusion that running for governor in 1928 probably would not be in their best interests. Hoover most certainly would win the presidency and in all likelihood would be reelected four years later. With this mixture of admiration and fear for Hoover, the decision was made to keep some distance from campaigns indefinitely and wait for the Democratic party to strengthen.

The 1928 Democratic Convention, held in Houston that summer, was not the most memorable for the party and reinforced Roosevelt's new plans. There was little competition for the presidential nomination, mainly because most potential candidates expected a defeat for the party in the fall. Al Smith was elected on the first ballot, and the Democrats hailed this turn of events as an indication that the divisiveness that had plagued the party for years finally was giving way to more unity. However, this image of unity could not be further from the truth. Although Smith enjoyed strong support in the northeast and in northern cities, his candidacy generated hostility in the south and in rural America—even among Democrats. Smith was a Catholic; he also openly opposed Prohibition. Neither of these facts played well in the conservative, Protestant-oriented and "dry" South and Midwest. Nevertheless, Roosevelt again played a significant role in promoting his fellow New Yorker and announced his nomination at the convention.

The harsh response sparked by Smith's nomination surprised Roosevelt, who may have underestimated the size and strength of the conservative wing of his party. Over the next few months, while Smith campaigned against Hoover, many Democrats began launching wild accusations about the New Yorker. One rumor claimed that Smith was an alcoholic. A southern fundamentalist minister warned that, as a Catholic, Smith would be controlled by the Pope. Extreme voices encouraged even more sinister rumors regarding Smith's immoral activities. The campaign in some ways brought out some of the worst elements of the Democratic party and perhaps represented a low point in its history. The Republicans, in contrast, ran a quiet, confident campaign while their opponents came apart at the seams.

If anything, the course of the campaign reinforced Roosevelt's inclination to avoid a run for elective office that year. However, shortly after the convention, party leaders began to place pressure on him to run for governor as a replacement for Smith. The idea had its appeal, because Smith, for whom Roosevelt had genuine respect, had won handily only two years earlier. Adding more pressure, Smith contacted Roosevelt directly about the decision, declaring that no one else could be a legitimate successor in Albany. Smith also ignored the forecasts of a Republican landslide in his own race and believed that the Democrats were in a position to pull off a surprise triumph nationally. Yet his own victory, he explained to Roosevelt, depended on victory in the governor's race as a means of delivering votes from their home state in the national election.

There was clear consensus among everybody close to Roosevelt that he should avoid running for office. Howe reminded him that losing the election, a very real possibility, would run counter to the plans they had laid out for the next several years. Still the pressure increased, as a tidal wave of letters, phone calls, and visitors descended on Hyde Park. Roosevelt continued firm in his refusal. Eleanor, Howe, and Sara all supported him.

Day after day of discussing the race began to take its toll on him. One prominent Democrat even offered to help him with the financing of the Warm Springs resort if he would do his duty for the party. Others worked to show him that the election was far from a lost cause, offering scenarios of narrow victories through winning key counties. Soon he began to vacillate and indicated that he might be willing to run. Almost immediately, party operatives leaked to the press that Roosevelt would be their candidate. As these events unfolded, the mood in Hyde Park was less than enthusiastic. Eleanor, who was traveling at this time, cabled him offering "regrets" regarding the news. Howe clearly was unhappy, and Missy Le-Hand evidently announced her hope that he would lose the election if he ran. All of them, however, knew that Roosevelt's mind already had been made up. Yet the typical Roosevelt enthusiasm was missing from his own voice. "Well, I've got to run for governor," he was said to have remarked on one occasion. "There's no use in all of us getting sick about it."

Compared to his previous campaigns, Roosevelt ran a half-hearted and unorganized campaign. The team assembled for him by the state party, however, was a good one. Howe and LeHand of course would work at his side, now with a new member, a young attorney named Samuel I. Rosen-man who had a background in progressive social causes. Roosevelt was impressed with his energy and commitment to detail. Often he showed up at Hyde Park with reams of statistics on a variety of issues. As the campaign moved forward, Rosenman helped assemble almost all of his policy statements. Another newcomer was James A. Farley, a young Democratic party secretary and close friend of Henry Morgenthau, along with secretary Grace Tully, who also became a fixture in the Roosevelt circle for years to come.

In fact, the party was better organized than Roosevelt may have imagined. A Tammany operative, Edward J. Flynn, worked behind the scenes to deliver the New York City vote, which allowed Roosevelt to concentrate his efforts on upstaters, who would be the toughest to attract. The entire team traveled in a caravan of cars and buses across rural New York, stopping in small town after small town to deliver stump speeches. As the campaign gathered momentum, Roosevelt's spirits picked up. At the start of things, there remained some concern as to whether he was prepared to meet the physical demands of a campaign. Those concerns quickly were dispelled as Roosevelt rediscovered the energy that had marked his previous campaigns.

While reporters focused on his health, wondering whether he was up to the demands of the campaign, Roosevelt worked to focus the race on issues. The Republicans, sensing the popularity of their presidential candidate, ran a cautious campaign designed to ride Hoover's coattails. Their candidate, State Attorney General Albert Ottinger, in fact, informed voters of his intentions to "Hooverize" the election. Democrats complained that there was more discussion of the presidential contest than local issues, and posters tended to feature Hoover rather than Ottinger.

In an attempt to draw a clear contrast between himself and his opponent, Roosevelt portrayed himself as a progressive reformer. He pledged to promote new legislation to aid struggling farmers, increase funding for schools, improve the standing of organized labor, and to devote more resources to build infrastructure. In some speeches, he moved even further to the left, calling for increased funding for child welfare and aid to widowed mothers. Voters had a clear choice in the election, as Ottinger echoed the Republican party's national campaign that championed lower taxes and pledged to scale back government regulation of the economy.

On election day, Roosevelt returned to Hyde Park to cast his vote, then spent the remainder of the day in New York City, where he awaited the returns at his campaign headquarters in the Biltmore Hotel. There was a much reason for pessimism, as Republicans enjoyed sweeping victories throughout the country, even in historically Democratic areas. Hoover's victory over Smith was stunning: 440 electoral votes to only 87—the most lopsided presidential contest in U.S. history. To add insult to injury, Hoover even carried the state of New York.

Roosevelt's own defeat then was a foregone conclusion, a sentiment shared by many newspaper editorialists who predicted a Republican sweep in New York in the days leading up to the election. Yet, as the returns began to trickle in, the voting was much closer than expected. As midnight struck at the end of election day, the race still was too close to call. The following day, word arrived that Roosevelt had won a photo finish— less than one-half of one percent of the voting had placed him over the top. His victory stood as a morsel of good news for a Democratic party that had little to celebrate that year and may have been the greatest electoral achievement of his career. If there had been any doubt that Roosevelt was now the national standard-bearer for the party, these were put to rest.

An exhausted but jubilant Roosevelt family then prepared for life in Albany. On December 31, 1928, he and Eleanor were received warmly by Smith at the governor's mansion in front of a throng of reporters and supporters. The entire family moved to the state capital. The boys were now away at school, but all considered the large, ornate, and somewhat stuffy structure their new home. Roosevelt was delighted with the turn of events, because, although the timing was a bit off, he always considered the state governorship an important step in his political career. Now he could contemplate with seriousness a campaign for the presidency—a plan that he discussed with his friends and close associates on several occasions.

Of course, there was a great deal of work to do for New York in the meantime, and Roosevelt settled into his new position quickly. Among the first tasks was to build an administrative team. Not surprisingly, he selected for most positions individuals with whom he had worked closely in getting to Albany. Ed Flynn, who had been most responsible for winning in New York City, became secretary of state, and Samuel Rosenman became the governor's chief counsel. Henry Morganthau would serve as chairman of an agricultural advising committee. LeHand and Tully were brought in as secretaries. Although it was important to assemble his own team, Roosevelt did tap some members of Smith's former administration, most notably Frances Perkins, who became head of the Department of Labor.

One conspicuous absence from Albany was Louis Howe, who saw little he could do there. Instead, he alternated between Hyde Park and New York City to work as Roosevelt's chief campaign strategist. James Farley, now head of the state party, worked with Howe not only to ensure a Roosevelt reelection two years down the road, but also to lay the groundwork for a presidential campaign should the opportunity arise in the future.

The new governor's challenges were not exactly formidable. There would be no need for a drastic altering of the status quo, because the state's economy was in good shape and Roosevelt shared the views of his predecessor. In fact, he saw as his greatest concern the need to establish himself as an independent leader and to step out of the shadow of Al Smith. At times this generated some stress between the two men, as Smith had expected to be a mentor to the new governor and to play an active role in the administration. Roosevelt, in his first experience in an executive office, tried to keep his distance and to cultivate an image of an independent leader. Over time their relationship cooled to the point that Smith would become something of a problem.

As governor, Roosevelt's political philosophy increasingly became a question for the public, both within New York and in other parts of the country. Above all, he considered himself a product of the Progressive Era. He maintained the view that government, at all levels, should be an active agent in bringing about positive social change. He continued to carry with him antimonopoly tendencies from his days in the Wilson administration and operated on the assumption that unregulated corporate power undermined democracy. However, he never had been a populist in the William Jennings Bryan mold. His wartime experience left with him a view that government and business were at their best when working together; in fact, several biographers have described Roosevelt's views on economics as in the tradition of Alexander Hamilton, who as the first secretary of the Treasury of the United States had promoted a vision of government working to enhance the productivity of American business rather than seeking to hinder its growth. He also believed that government regulation could improve economic efficiency by encouraging constructive competition.

This ethos of cooperation between government and private industry mirrored his views on organized labor—views also shaped during World War I. Far from being a radical, Roosevelt understood trade unions as a means for workers to improve their lives. From a political standpoint, he also came to the view that labor was a potentially valuable constituency because of the ability of unions to mobilize the rank and file. The war also had taught Roosevelt that labor organizations could hinder prosperity and that union leaders could be as guilty of self-aggrandizement as business leaders. As a Progressive, he believed that labor and government were not by necessity opposed in their aims, and that cooperation could benefit workers and industry. He would learn while governor of New York that labor could be a powerful political force for the Democratic party.

Like most Progressives, Roosevelt saw a close link between an enhanced role for government and the growth of democracy. Good government, he believed, was rooted in mass participation. Government was not antagonistic to the people; rather, it was an extension of the people and should be viewed as a force for public good against powerful interests. There was, of course, a patrician element in Roosevelt's view of government, for the well-to-do in his view had a responsibility to improve the livelihood of the less-fortunate. Such sentiments were reinforced in his early days as a state legislator, when he viewed his fights with Tammany as a war between power brokers and the common man. Roosevelt's populism seemed to swing back and forth between industrial workers and rural Americans. For the most part, he viewed U.S. society in terms of economic class—the lower orders required representation in government to combat the wealthy.

These political attitudes were just that—general views rather than a clear set of philosophic tendencies. Roosevelt often was described as a pragmatist because of his willingness to experiment with various reforms. Certainly he was not an ideologue. Roosevelt never had been fond of philosophy and was not in any way an intellectual. If anything, he was altogether typical of most Americans. Dedicated to vague ideals of democracy, freedom, and the free market, he was more concerned with outcomes rather than fitting policies and programs into a theoretical framework. Intellectuals of all stripes at times would voice their frustration with his leadership. As governor, and later as president, he approached issues singularly, rather than as part of a larger theoretical design.

His first major challenge as governor was a battle with the Republican-controlled legislature over the state budget. During his first months as governor, Roosevelt received advice from a small army of advisors on a range of issues. When finally assembled, it was perhaps the most ambitious spending plan in the state's history. He sought to make changes in several areas, including increased spending for health care facilities, more funding for schools, parks, and highways. In all, his proposals called for a significant increase in spending from previous years. Even a number of Democrats in the legislature were surprised by the amount of reform spending he proposed in his first budget. From the start, opponents made clear their intentions to block its passage.

There was a great deal at stake in the budget war. For one thing, in the prior legislative session the entire budgetary process had been changed. For the first time, the governor rather than the legislature would create a budget, which would then be submitted to the assembly for approval—a change that clearly gave the governor much more power to determine spending priorities. Roosevelt was the first governor to operate under these new rules; the legislature, particularly the Republican leadership, saw the budgetary process as crucial in setting a precedent. They had no intention of allowing their role in the process to be diminished and sent clear signals to the governor that nothing would be rubber-stamped.

The other issue had to with how Roosevelt drew up his budget. Rather than establishing particular amounts of spending for each individual program, the budget requested lump sums for general areas of reform. His explanation was that many of the details of his program were to be worked out over the following year. These spending allotments were estimates, and the expectation was that once monies were secured, then the administration would begin developing clear plans to spend them. Leaders in the legislature rejected a great deal of the budget and returned to Roosevelt's office a counter-proposal with several items deleted or cut down. Roosevelt vetoed the amended budget, and eventually the matter found its way into the state courts.

The battle over the budget, which Roosevelt eventually won, was significant on several fronts. For one, Roosevelt proved to be a strong leader and was willing to take the fight to his opponents. In fact, much to their consternation, Roosevelt actually seemed energized by the debate. At one point he described the affair as a "grand little fight with the legislature." Also significant was Roosevelt's willingness to go directly to the public over the issue. During the heated deliberations, the governor went to the airwaves with radio addresses in support of his reforms. Although the impact of the speeches was difficult to determine, he came away from the experience convinced that a direct appeal to the people could yield results and that the radio was an ideal way to reach them. For the remainder of the year Roosevelt continued to jab with the legislature over various proposals.

Roosevelt's first term as governor sailed along until the following autumn, when the entire nation was rocked by the stock market crash. On October 24, 1929, otherwise known as "black Tuesday," the nation's economy trembled as the stock market tumbled downward. Two days later, the bottom dropped out, as stock values fell to levels not seen in years. Although no one knew it at the time, the Great Crash was about to usher in the longest and most severe economic depression in the nation's history. The decade-long crisis transformed the U.S. political scene; it certainly changed the trajectory of Franklin Roosevelt's career.

There had been warning signs that the stock market had inflated to potentially dangerous levels. Years of productivity, particularly in the manufacturing sectors of the economy, yielded steadily increasing stock values through the mid-1920s. Amidst this long-term bull market, investment banks loosened the reigns on credit with which to buy stocks; the result was a boom in stock purchases made on borrowed money. For several years, easy money was to be had for both investors and banks, as soaring stock prices generated dividends that could be used to buy even more stock. This financial house of cards had started to raise concerns years prior to the crash. President Hoover, during his first year in office, attempted to slow down the charging bull to no avail. When the decline came, it came quickly as investors who carried large debts tried to sell out before the bottom dropped out. Some did; most did not and not only lost fortunes but faced enormous loans as well. Banks, now feeling the pains of overextension, tried to call in their loans but found bankrupt investors on the other end. The entire financial system began to grind to a halt.

Stock market crashes were not new, and in the days and weeks following the initial disaster all attention focused on a quick recovery. With the aid of hindsight, however, it was clear that the economy of the Roaring Twenties was built on a number of shaky foundations that the stock market crash only served to expose more fully. Farmers had been struggling with low prices, mainly due to overproduction, since the end of World War I. Similarly, by the end of the decade, several areas of manufacturing were facing slumps as the marketplace became saturated with products. Prices across the board had begun to dip late in the decade, creating serious problems for businesses. If prices fell too low, layoffs would be the result as profits dwindled. In the months following the crash, unemployment began creeping up as this scenario played itself out.

The international situation did not help matters. Overproduction of U.S. food and manufactured goods might have been handled by increasing exports—buyers overseas could purchase products that Americans could not, thus keeping prices up. The problem lay in the fact that the economies of Europe, which received the majority of American exports, also were stagnating. To make matters even worse, many countries in Europe relied on loans from American banks to make ends meet; increased purchasing power overseas then required more funds from banks in the United States, which were running out of capital. It was a vicious and downward spiral with disastrous results not only in the United States, but in Europe and around the globe.

In the early aftermath of the crash, Roosevelt echoed the sentiments of most Americans that the incident simply was a "correction" to an inflated market and would mostly impact high-level financiers. In Washington, Hoover saw no need for panic. Attempting to assure the public that the economy remained strong, he called on business leaders to do everything possible to avoid cutting jobs. In a series of speeches, Hoover maintained that renewed prosperity was just around the corner—words that would haunt him over the next three years as the economy continued to drag.

Back in New York, Roosevelt watched these events with concern. By the summer of 1930 the state's economy had begun to exhibit the slowdown happening nationwide. Yet the slump was gradual and few people anticipated the magnitude of the Great Depression. Interestingly, the economy was not a major issue in Roosevelt's bid for reelection that year. Even as unemployment continued to creep upward throughout the summer, Roosevelt calmly assured voters that no drastic action was necessary. His behavior may be explained in part by the fact that, as a governor facing an upcoming election, there was certainly no reason to focus on economic woes for which he himself could be held responsible in the eyes of voters.

The election that fall turned out to be a landslide for Roosevelt as he stressed throughout the campaign the accomplishments of his first term. He received twice the number of votes that Al Smith had won in any of his victorious campaigns of the previous decade. More significant was the fact that, while Roosevelt downplayed the economic situation, voters across the country had begun to notice. The year was a strong one for the Democratic party, in New York and elsewhere. In Washington, the party gained seats in the Senate and took control of the House of Representatives. Public opinion was beginning to turn sharply against Hoover, which offered Democrats the surprising possibility of upending him in the next election. Even with the economy in a dire position, the chances of returning a Democrat to the White House for the first time in over a decade would not be easy. A victory required someone with a solid record of achievement; someone with political momentum, and the verve to reconstruct the political landscape. Franklin Roosevelt would be that man.

Chapter 7

VICTORY

Franklin Roosevelt's campaign for the presidency began in earnest in 1930, fully two years before the election. Following his landslide reelection victory as governor of New York that year, editorials appeared in newspapers across the country identifying him as the probable nominee to challenge President Hoover. Even the usually cautious Louis Howe, who never left anything to chance, told a group of reporters that Roosevelt's nomination was all but assured, remarking that, "even if no one should raise a finger about it," the race would be handed to his boss. Such a statement, out of character for Howe, indicated their confidence in the wake of their most recent triumph.

One source of confidence was the fact that few Democrats across the country had the momentum that Roosevelt carried out of the midterm elections. Timing and careful planning had been a key component of his political career, and Howe, Farley, and Roosevelt himself began to see that the hour had struck. Over the next several months, while Roosevelt focused on his work in Albany, Howe and Farley began laying the groundwork to secure the nomination by contacting party leaders in various states. Despite their newfound confidence, nothing could be left to chance.

The dramatic events of the past year had transformed the political landscape. The seemingly untouchable Hoover floundered as the economy limped along despite assurances of prosperity around the corner. At times, there were signs of hope, as some economic indicators occasionally hinted at a recovery only to again turn downward. By 1930, hundreds of banks had closed their doors, and the number grew into the thousands over the next two years. Unemployment also continued its upward trek; at its peak, 25 percent of the American public was without a job. In some parts of the country, the number reached 50 percent.

Before the Great Depression began, most Americans would have been encouraged to know that Herbert Hoover would be their president during a time of economic crisis. Known for combining a humanitarian impulse with the sharp mind of an engineer, he had gained from World War I an image of being a problem solver. Yet as the economy moved into its second, and then third, year of sluggishness, the cautious and staid Hoover began to take on the image of a "do-nothing" president.

The tragedy for Hoover was that the administration was doing a great deal to stem the tide of the Depression. In keeping with his Progressive philosophy, he turned to both expert opinion and cooperative efforts between the government and the private sector to map out a strategy to turn things around. Among the more notable reforms was the creation of the Reconstruction Finance Corporation, designed to pump funds into failing banks and industries. Large loans also were offered to farmers to help with collapsing prices and mounting debt. Hoover believed the Depression was a structural problem. Rather than focusing on relief efforts, he thought it best to place greater effort in addressing the overall organization of the economy. He also was convinced that the roots of the crisis lay in the international financial situation and addressed the imbalance in global trade that seemed to encourage the dismal economy.

Hoover's aloof demeanor and mild confidence had been suited perfectly for a pre-Depression nation that had enjoyed years of prosperity. Now, however, that persona seemed to imply that he was out of touch with reality and lacked concern for the plight of people suffering from unemployment. He did care a great deal, but Hoover was not the sort of political leader who would clasp hands with farmers and blue-collar workers and show empathy for their plight. In his view, the Depression would have to be solved in Washington and on Wall Street. In the meantime, Americans would have to tighten their belts and ride out the storm.

By this time Roosevelt was beginning to face his own share of difficulties in meeting the demands of a concerned public. The number of unemployed New Yorkers pushed beyond one million; bank failures swept through Wall Street and across the state like aftershocks of an earthquake. As much at a loss as Hoover regarding how to respond, he called members of his cabinet together to design programs that might turn things around. In the first months of his second term, Roosevelt seemed willing to talk to anyone who might have fresh ideas.

Historians have made much of the differences in political philosophy between Hoover and Roosevelt and the way they approached the Depression. There actually were more similarities than differences. Both assumed that the government would play a role in recovery. Both leaned heavily on expert opinion to develop policy. Both understood that, while steps might be taken to alleviate the crisis, there was no need to contemplate a fundamental reordering of the U.S. economy. Both men also were conservative in fearing that increases in government spending might trigger budget deficits.

There was a difference between them regarding unemployment relief programs. Hoover had considered offering federally funded relief to people who had lost jobs but rejected such policies as a "dole" that ran counter to the ethos of American individualism and the ideal of self-sustenance. While Washington could provide funds for structural recovery, loans to business and banks, and even create employment projects for those out of work, Hoover maintained that relief payments violated basic values of the country. Yet there were points of agreement between the two men. Hoover was not opposed to unemployment insurance systems created at the state level and, in fact, called on governors across the country to adopt them. In New York, Roosevelt's creation of a Temporary Emergency Relief Administration, which earmarked millions of dollars in direct unemployment aid, was consistent with Hoover's approach to the Depression. There was a difference in emphasis, however. While Hoover seemed to be dragged into supporting government action, Roosevelt embraced the opportunity for experimentation. During a special session of the state legislature, Roosevelt delivered an address in person that urged the government to become the focal point of recovery and relief. Here his paternalistic nature emerged, as he said of the unemployed that, "to those unfortunate citizens aid must be extended by government—not as a matter of charity but as a matter of social duty."

Roosevelt had to balance a sincere concern for offering assistance to those in need with political calculation. Republicans in Albany were not standing idle and had advanced their own programs. In some ways, there was a tug-of-war over who would control relief. A bill that called for the creation of a legislative committee to oversee relief was attacked by Roosevelt as too extravagant. The real issue, however, was where authority lay and who would receive credit. In some respects the battle over relief mirrored the battles over budgetary matters of Roosevelt's first term.

Following reelection Roosevelt assembled a team of advisors to create new programs, a group that would receive fame in Washington as the

"Brain Trust." Some of the team members were old hands, such as Howe. Now Frances Perkins became a key advisor, along with Harry L. Hopkins, an energetic and rough-hewn social worker who became head of the Temporary Emergency Relief Administration. Others who arrived in Albany to work at Roosevelt's side included Columbia University professor Raymond Moley and economists Rexford Tugwell and Adolf Berle. By 1932, the group had formed into a fairly tight-knit circle and met regularly with Roosevelt. Their conversations, formal and informal, ran the gamut, from mundane matters of politics to broader philosophic considerations. To the degree that Roosevelt left the governorship with a set of refined principles regarding the Depression, these were shaped by this team.

By the beginning of the election year, Roosevelt was hailed by Democrats around the country as the most proactive governor in addressing the Depression. The administration could point to an impressive list of programs and initiatives designed to offer relief and recovery, despite the fact that the economy in New York had improved little, if at all. At the same time, his repeated calls for a balanced budget undercut accusations of extremism. With little surprise, he gave his approval to appear on the primary ballot in North Dakota in January, officially launching his campaign.

Although he was the clear front-runner in New York, there were several challenges to be addressed at home before focusing on a national contest. One problem was the surprising amount of antagonism that had erupted between Roosevelt and Al Smith. Part of the rift had to do with policy. The former governor announced his disagreement with a number of Roosevelt's spending programs. Perhaps the main reason, however, was that Smith had felt spurned by the administration. New York had been Smith's state for a decade, and he considered Roosevelt his heir and something of a protégé, a sentiment never shared by Roosevelt. From the outset, Roosevelt distanced himself from his predecessor to avoid the image of being a Smith crony, a move that Smith considered a rebuff. Fears that Smith would try to influence the new administration became evident when he disclosed his plans to live in Albany after his unsuccessful run for the presidency. Even Eleanor warned that Smith could be a problem if the public came to view her husband as nothing more than a puppet of the elder statesman.

Another obstacle was William Randolph Hearst, the newspaper mogul who continued to cast a long shadow over the Democratic party in New York. Hearst had been a thorn in Roosevelt's side since World War I. A strong proponent of unilateralism, he had been a major voice of opposition to the League of Nations and used his influence in the press to defeat the Senate treaty that would have brought the United States into the organization. Now that Roosevelt emerged as the Democratic front-runner, Hearst again went on the attack and portrayed him as an erratic internationalist who would undermine the country's autonomy in foreign policy. The controversy must have irritated Roosevelt, who really felt as though the League had become a dead issue. However, he also understood the power Hearst held in the media and knew that he had to respond to the criticism. Left unchecked, he might support another candidate, such as conservative John Nance Garner of Texas, conceivably driving a wedge into the Democratic party. To secure the nomination, Roosevelt understood the need for a unified New York delegation at the convention.

Hearst's challenge required some maneuvering. Seeking middle ground, Roosevelt backtracked on his support for the League by stating that the League had, over the years, shown itself to be ineffective by deviating from Wilson's original design. When asked directly if the United States should join, he answered in the negative. This change of heart may have dealt effectively with Hearst, but it generated new problems. The columnist Walter Lippmann, a respected voice across the nation, interpreted Roosevelt's shift as an indication of shallowness and lack of resolve. In a stinging column that would be repeated and reprinted by Roosevelt opponents for years to come, Lippmann described him as a political opportunist who lacked any real conviction. "Franklin D. Roosevelt is no crusader," he summarized at the end of the piece. "He is no tribune of the people. He is no enemy of entrenched privilege. He is a pleasant man who, without any qualifications for the office, would very much like to be president."

Lippmann's sneer certainly was not the first time, nor the last, that an intellectual would be frustrated by a political figure's lack of consistency. The attack, however, was merely a bump in the road; and, at any rate, the main challenge was to win the nomination, not the hearts and minds of the editorialists. He was the clear favorite entering the convention, which was held in Chicago in late June. There were hurdles, including a bloc of delegates who launched an ill-fated "Stop Roosevelt" movement from the floor of the convention. When the balloting began, Roosevelt was well ahead but just short of the two-thirds required to win. There was some concern that if the opposition held firm for several successive voting rounds, the convention would move to locate a compromise candidate. Among the holdouts was the Texas delegation, led by the savvy Sam Rayburn, who continued to press for their favorite son, Garner. The Roosevelt team had planned for this move; Farley managed to convince the Texans to release their delegates to Roosevelt in exchange for Garner being placed on the ticket as the running mate.

Holding to tradition, Roosevelt had remained in Hyde Park during the proceedings while Farley and Howe worked to secure the nomination. When he received the good news, Roosevelt boarded a plane and arrived in Chicago to offer his acceptance speech to an enthusiastic crowd. He spoke briefly on recovery and relief programs he had supported in New York that became the basis for the party's platform. Most notably, he explained that, if elected, he planned to offer the country a "new deal" to overcome the Depression and revive the confidence of the American people. The phrase had not been designed as a campaign slogan, but it appeared in headlines across the country the following day, prompting the party to adopt it as an official slogan.

Once again the Roosevelts prepared for an exhausting campaign. Eleanor grumbled early on about the prospects of moving to the White House and being placed in "captivity" as the first lady. Yet despite such reservations, she launched into the race and became a key member of the team. She oversaw activities of the National Democratic Committee's women's division and plotted a course for organizing women in states that she referred to as "fighting states." Her willingness to deliver public addresses on behalf of her husband was an innovation in campaigning, and more than a few observers found her actions improper. Much more than Franklin, she balanced her optimism for victory with concerns about the enormous responsibilities that her husband faced should he win the election. The entire nation seemed to expect Roosevelt to take on the Depression single-handedly. Her hesitancy was not so much an indication of a lack of confidence in his abilities but rather a well-founded consideration of the real depth of the economic crisis.

If Roosevelt shared any of her concerns, he never showed them. His entry into the campaign was akin to the proverbial fish into water. He crisscrossed the country, alternating between brief appearances and making longer, more substantial speeches. At times the journey became a literal whistle-stop campaign, as his train, dubbed the "Roosevelt Special," would pull into stations and allow him to appear at the back to greet onlookers for only a minute or two. Then the train would push on to the next station, with Roosevelt beaming and waving furiously as the crowd of onlookers watched it disappear.

The campaign strategy, designed primarily by Farley and Howe with Rosenman doing most of the speechwriting, alternated between attacks on Hoover and outlines of Roosevelt's plans. In speech after speech, Roo-

sevelt hammered away at the president; at times he described the administration as the "Four Horsemen"—the horsemen of Destruction, Delay,
Deceit, and Despair. He accused Hoover of enacting policies that encouraged overproduction and misleading the public about the severity of the
Depression. He also painted a portrait of Hoover as an inactive and un-
caring figure who refused to help those suffering from unemployment and
poverty.

Hoover's actions during the election year did little to advance his own
cause. His image as a cool, sober thinker had devolved into one of a craven
and unresponsive leader. He lacked the charisma displayed by Roosevelt.
Public criticism of his leadership reached a crescendo during the campaign season. The term "Hoovervilles" had emerged to describe shanty
communities that sprang up on the outskirts of some cities, inhabited by
the chronically poor. Songs of the period often described the state of the
economy, such as the smash success of "Brother Can You Spare a Dime?"
In some respects Roosevelt did not have to campaign strenuously; the past
few years served as condemnation of the incumbent president that often
was more effective than anything the Democrats could offer.

The bungling of the so-called Bonus Army, which occurred during
the campaign season, perhaps finished off any chance that Hoover had
at reelection. The incident began a year earlier, when a group of World
War I veterans launched a crusade to receive their pensions that were
not to come due for several more years. The movement had gained momentum throughout the spring, and in July some twenty thousand men
descended on Washington to protest the administration's silence on the
issue. Camps of men, housed in shanties and tents, spread across the Ana-
costia Flats across from the Capitol; each day the men took to the streets
in calm demonstrations to place pressure on the government to deliver
payments. Although on the whole the protestors were well behaved, the
situation understandably raised fears of mob violence or, at the very least,
incidents of crime.

In what Hoover hoped would end the controversy, he encouraged a bill
through Congress approving payment on the pensions, a measure he was
certain would not pass. When it was indeed rejected, most of the protestors
departed Washington, except for a few thousand more militant individuals
who refused to budge. Attempting to clear up the mess, Hoover ordered
the military to force the holdouts out of the city, a task handed over to
Major George S. Patton, who swept through the Flats with a large cavalry
force. What occurred then was a fiasco, as many of the men burned their
shacks and prepared for violence. As the flames and smoke spread across

the city, Hoover beamed that "a challenge to the authority of the United States government has been met, swiftly and firmly." While perhaps true, Hoover's actions also became a public relations nightmare, as newspapers across the country wrote blistering accounts of the president's callousness and complete withdrawal from the plight of the suffering. In the wake of the incident, some Republicans began to suggest that it would be best if Hoover removed himself from the ticket to avoid further damage.

Given this situation, Roosevelt believed that the best strategy would be to coast to victory by avoiding offering specific proposals that might be open to ridicule by the opposition. While most of his speeches offered little more than platitudes about restoring hope and confidence, he did hint at some of the policies the new administration might pursue. There would be attempts to address overproduction, both in agriculture and industry. He spoke in favor of increased public works and promised direct action to provide relief for the unemployed. Consistent with his experience in New York, he assured voters that government spending would not increase and that the federal budget would remain in balance. At times his message even sounded more like that of Hoover discussing the need for people to take responsibility for their own predicaments by working harder and living more frugally. Hoover, on the defensive, attempted to portray Roosevelt as a radical who sought to place the nation onto a path of revolution. With ideas, according to Hoover, that bore "the fumes of the witch's cauldron which boiled in Russia," he warned that Roosevelt "would destroy the very foundations of our American system." Such dire rhetoric smacked of desperation, which it was. Efforts to portray Roosevelt as a Bolshevik had little impact on the electorate. In fact, in terms of proposals there were few differences among the two campaigns. What distinguished them was style rather than substance.

As Roosevelt finished up his final campaign stops and returned to New York, he was confident of victory. Breaking from routine, he spent Election Day waiting for returns in New York City at Democratic party headquarters rather than in Hyde Park. As the hours passed, a crowd of supporters formed outside the office ready to celebrate the outcome. Early in the evening Roosevelt emerged, thanking them and offering thanks to his team.

The numbers that began to roll in were overwhelming. Roosevelt received over 57 percent of the popular vote and trounced Hoover in the electoral college 472 to 59, as the incumbent carried only six states. That evening, while returns continued to come in, Roosevelt visited his mother at her home in lower Manhattan. As he embraced her, flanked by his family, he was said to have declared, "This is the greatest night of my life." Even Sara, who in the past had complained about his chosen career path, was quite proud of her son. Eleanor too was happy for him, for she knew that he had achieved his life's goal. As he took stock of the situation that evening, after the celebrations had calmed, he must have been aware of the awesome responsibility that lay before him. The nation had spoken with a clear voice that they wanted Roosevelt; now he was expected to deliver.

Chapter 8

LAUNCHING THE NEW DEAL

Franklin Roosevelt stood solemnly on a platform in the capital plaza as a cold wind swept through the gathered crowd. The day was March 4, 1933, and Roosevelt had just been sworn in as the 32nd president of the United States. The day had gone exactly as planned. Following church services on this Saturday morning, a motorcade had made its way to the White House to pick up the outgoing president and first lady; Roosevelt and Hoover, who long since had destroyed any warmth that might have made the short trip to the inaugural ceremony more celebratory, sat in silence. The day was filled with anticipation, not just in Washington but all across the nation, as Americans for months had yearned for some indication that change was coming. Roosevelt's speech to those gathered in Washington, and also in front of radios everywhere, was a blend of urgency and optimism. "This great nation will endure as it has endured," he announced with a dramatic cadence. "The only thing we have to fear is fear itself."

The words offered a glimpse into the pervasive helplessness that marked the national mood. Eleanor remembered later that the sight of the gathered throng was somewhat unnerving: "You felt that they would do *anything*—only if someone told them *what* to do." Roosevelt was at his best that day. He assured Americans that "the nation asks for action, and action now." He went further to compare the Great Depression to war, calling for unity and a renewed sense of national purpose to confront the crisis.

Ironically, the path to the White House may have been more arduous after the election than before. Anxious to prepare for the upcoming transfer of power, Roosevelt had assembled a transition team and sought to confer with Hoover on matters of foreign and domestic policy. Yet meaningful collaboration between the two was doomed from the start. Hoover, still hurting by the harshness of the campaign and the overwhelming opposition to his reelection, remained defensive and convinced himself that Roosevelt had nothing constructive to offer the nation during this lame-duck period of months between the election and the inauguration. He also believed his campaign rhetoric, that the last hope for the country lay in the adoption of his policies rather than those of his opponent, whom he considered to be an extremist. Hoover truly believed that the United States was about to embark upon a disastrous path.

Their meetings during these months were a clash of personality and ideas. Hoover made clear from the outset that he had no plans to confer with his successor. Believing that Roosevelt was in over his head, Hoover expected his role to be that of a mentor or teacher. He also believed Roosevelt's approach to the Depression was full of innocence and empty idealism. Roosevelt, for his part, entered their first meeting with a view that the election was an indication that Americans wanted change. Where Hoover was willing to help, Roosevelt would accept, but he felt little need to be instructed on matters. Their few encounters were wholly unproductive and were described by observers as awkward.

Another set of events was much more harrowing than dealing with the moody Hoover. In February, while visiting Miami, Roosevelt was the victim of an assassination attempt. Joseph Zangara, an unstable man who claimed to hate politicians, fired five shots at the president-elect in a city park. Roosevelt came away without injury; however, Chicago mayor Anton Cermak was killed in the attack. According to those present, Roosevelt displayed an almost eerie calmness throughout the ordeal and took control of the situation amidst a great deal of panic. If the incident bothered him at all, he refused to show it. In the wake of the tragedy, most around him agreed that extra personal security would be a good idea; Roosevelt refused this out-of-hand. He mentioned the shooting very seldom in later years; with time most Americans forgot about the affair.

With these trying events swirling, he and his advisors worked furiously to design an economic recovery program that could be implemented immediately following the inauguration. With respect to the international situation, he met with foreign policy experts from the Wilson administration, members of Congress involved with foreign affairs, and members of Hoover's foreign affairs staff. On domestic issues, the list of advisors who came through Roosevelt's doors was even greater. Raymond Moley assembled much of the group, which included Henry Morgenthau, Rexford

Tugwell, and a young editor from Nebraska named Henry Wallace. This foursome addressed agricultural reform. Moley also helped to assemble a team focused on finance and industry that included William Woodin, who became Roosevelt's secretary of the treasury; Lewis Douglas, an energetic economist from Arizona; and several Wall Street financiers and bankers.

For weeks prior to the inauguration, these teams worked closely with Roosevelt and were crucial in defining the tone of the new administration. They also became a natural recruiting pool for his cabinet. His selections for key positions ran the intellectual gamut and came from all regions of the country; the one common trait they shared was support for Roosevelt during his run for the Democratic party nomination a year earlier. The main criteria seemed to be how well each would work under his authority. Cordell Hull of Tennessee, who had risen in the ranks of the party to become a senator, became secretary of state. Harold Ickes, a seasoned progressive reformer from Chicago with ties to the Theodore Roosevelt administration, was tapped for secretary of the interior. Henry Wallace, already hard at work on agricultural policy, would head the Department of Agriculture. Among the more notable selections was Frances Perkins, head of New York's Labor Department under Roosevelt, who became secretary of labor—the first woman in U.S. history to hold a cabinet-level position.

The new president also had every intention to rely heavily on members of his inner circle who had contributed to his rise in politics. Louis Howe took on the duties of chief secretary. Jim Farley, who had worked brilliantly at the Democratic party convention on Roosevelt's behalf, was awarded with the position of postmaster general. Steve Early, who had been campaigning for Roosevelt since the 1920 run for vice president, would be in charge of relations with the press, becoming, in effect, the first press secretary for a president; later administrations would consider the position indispensable. Moley and Tugwell also found places in the administration; the former as an assistant secretary of state and the latter an assistant secretary of agriculture.

Given the diversity and size of the group that helped to formulate New Deal policy, it stood to reason that there would not be a strong ideological or philosophical framework for the administration. Roosevelt seemed to be open to all viewpoints and was more impressed with those who had innovative ideas that might generate results rather than advisors who came across as narrow in their thinking. His policies would at times seem inconsistent, haphazard, and even contradictory as a result of this decision-making style. The emphasis was on action, and often these advisors spent more time working to sell the president on their policies than actually designing them.

Despite Roosevelt's fondness for pomp and celebration, he avoided the usual fanfare surrounding a president's first day in the White House and instead plunged directly into work. He fully intended to assure the American public that his administration would act immediately; to do so, a great deal of preparation took place prior to the inauguration. The Brain Trust worked day and night leading up to that Saturday, and there was no intention of dampening the momentum. Roosevelt attended a parade after his acceptance speech and attended a dinner at the White House with the extended Roosevelt family. Afterward, however, he went to work; Eleanor and the rest of the family attended the various galas and balls that evening on his behalf while the team retreated to an office to roll up their sleeves and get started.

Part of the urgency was due to typical Roosevelt enthusiasm; another factor was public opinion. There was consensus within the brain trust that, given the national mood, the sight of the new president attending high-brow parties and celebrating gaily would set the wrong tone for the first months of the administration. Furthermore, events had been moving quickly in the days leading up to the inauguration that demanded immediate attention. Early in the evening, the entire cabinet took their oaths of office collectively in a White House office rather than in a public ceremony—another indication that the team intended to depart from protocol. Then the group, Roosevelt included, settled in for a long night of work.

The immediate issue was the condition of the banking system, which was degenerating to the point of disaster. Gold reserves, which had been declining gradually for months, plummeted in the days before Roosevelt took office and had reached the point that they barely could back the national currency. In some states, the situation had become so dire that all banking had been suspended indefinitely. Just days earlier, Hoover had met with financial advisors, including his secretary of the treasury, Ogden Mills, who suggested that the president declare a national "bank holiday" that would allow financial institutions to catch their breath. Hoover refused to do so, not because he disagreed with the idea but because he believed that Roosevelt should make the decision. In the evening before the inauguration, advisors for both presidents had worked into the morning hours planning for a nationwide shutdown of all banks.

There were two issues to be tackled. The most urgent was how to stem the tide of failing banks. The incoming secretary of the treasury, William

Wooding, along with Attorney General Homer Cummings, had worked out a plan to invoke the Trading with the Enemy Act, a law that had been in place since the late 1700s, to stop gold exports. Such a move would, in effect, shut down the banking system altogether. Unclear was whether this action would hold up in the Supreme Court as constitutional; Cummings assured his boss that he would back the idea, and the issue of constitutionality was moot because it would take days, perhaps weeks or months, for the Supreme Court to decide on the matter. On Sunday, the administration contacted banks and governors around the country to inform them that, at midnight, an order to close all banks would go into effect. The plan also called for the creation of an Emergency Banking Act to spell out the details of the action after the fact.

The bank holiday was Roosevelt's first policy decision as president—one that set the tone for his first months in office. The administration expected a firestorm in Congress, particularly from Republicans who would charge that the administration was running roughshod over the legislative process. Yet the frenetic pace of Roosevelt's staff caught his opponents off guard. Even before copies of the banking bill were printed, Democratic leaders were pushing the measure through the House of Representatives, passing around hand-written copies. On Thursday, March 9, only four days into Roosevelt's presidency, the bill passed the Senate by a vote of 73 to 7.

Critics complained that the Emergency Banking Act set a dangerous precedent by allowing the president to intervene in the economy at will. Roosevelt actually viewed the measure as moderate, considering that some within the brain trust concluded that the best way to confront the crisis was for the federal government to take over banks completely and thus nationalize the financial system. In its final design, banks would be compelled to close their doors until they could show stability in their reserves; for a large number of banks, the holiday lasted only one day. Those on more shaky ground, however, might be closed for weeks or months. The bill also allowed the United States Treasury to supply funds to banks with severe needs. Within a week, the vast majority of financial institutions around the country were again up and running.

The administration was concerned that freezing the banking system might set off a panic, and that as soon as banks reopened, depositors would rush in and pull every penny out. To combat this possibility, Roosevelt drew upon his experiences as governor of New York by using the airwaves to assure the nation that the banking system was sound. On Sunday night, less than 24 hours after being sworn in, and just two hours before the bank holiday was to go into effect on the East Coast, he broadcast an address to millions of listeners across the country. Despite the drama surrounding the decision, Roosevelt struck a calm demeanor by speaking not from his desk in the oval office but from a chair beside the fireplace. This "fireside chat," a tactic that had proven successful in New York, was the first of many during his time in the White House. He explained the problem in plain terms and assured Americans that their banks were safe. He also called on Americans to do their duty to combat the crisis by keeping their funds in place. Appealing to patriotism and unity, he closed the address with an admonition that "together we cannot fail." The first fireside chat was an unprecedented use of radio that served as an example for future presidents who sought to make use of mass media.

The bank holiday offered a short-term solution for the crisis, and there was widespread agreement within the brain trust that broader reform was necessary. Roosevelt turned to Houston-based financier Jesse H. Jones, who became head of the Reconstruction Finance Corporation, to oversee substantial changes in the banking system. For years there had been calls by financial experts for the federal government to develop a means for guaranteeing bank deposits while avoiding a complete government take-over. One idea was to use the free market, in coordination with the government, to bring about more stability. Banks would raise funds through the sale of preferred stock that would be funneled into a newly created Federal Deposit Insurance Corporation (FDIC) and be held as a reserve in the event of a bank failure, thus reassuring Americans that they could deposit their savings into banks without risking a complete loss in the event of a panic. Roosevelt, in the beginning, considered the plan too intrusive, but the reformers gradually won him over. The FDIC was launched in June; within six months Jones had built up over one billion dollars in capital that backed thousands of banks nationwide.

The creation of depositors' insurance provided more stability and confidence in the banking system; however, it did not address the root problem, which continued to be a dwindling U.S. gold supply. Here, international events were a factor. Great Britain had sent the U.S. economy into a tailspin when, a few years earlier, it had abandoned the gold standard as the basis for its currency. The impact of the decision was that the British pound, now no longer backed by gold, diminished in value, which increased prices on goods. The move also jump-started the economy as global investors began to prefer to deal in British pounds rather than the more expensive U.S. dollar. As a result, rumors abounded that the United States would soon follow Britain's lead, which encouraged speculators to purchase as much gold as possible in anticipation of the move. Hoover had opposed breaking from the gold standard; Roosevelt remained vague on the idea during the campaign. With Roosevelt's election, however, a large number of investors placed their bets on a move away from a gold-based currency.

A debate ensued within the administration. Inflation could be a positive for the economy, for rising prices could help ailing businesses. However, there also was fear that if the dollar were no longer backed by precious metal, its value would plummet and spark runaway inflation. In a way, however, the bank holiday already had set off a chain of events that rendered the gold standard obsolete. Once banks reopened, a frenzied purchase of U.S. gold ensued. Finally, on April 18, Roosevelt announced that the nation no longer was on the gold standard. The value of the U.S. dollar would now be determined by its status in the global economy rather than tied to the price, and quantity, of gold in the United States Treasury.

Although the decision did not come unexpectedly, there was considerable reaction. Many financiers were unhappy with the move, as the now devalued dollar meant that creditors would pay the price. One banker even declared that the abandonment of the gold standard was an indication that Western civilization was on the decline. Many Americans simply could not fathom a currency that did not have the backing of tangible metal. Yet the change did achieve its intended result, as the value of the dollar dropped significantly in the days following the announcement. The move also triggered mild inflation, because prices rose slightly as the value of the dollar declined. Although the changes were slight, Roosevelt could now point out that, for the first time since the stock market crash, there seemed to be visible growth in economic activity.

These financial considerations were but a small part of a flurry of legislation that poured out of the White House and onto the floor of Congress in the first months of Roosevelt's presidency, the so-called Hundred Days. In all, there were 15 significant acts, focused on a range of issues, that became law during the period. Roosevelt enjoyed extraordinary success in gaining approval for his proposals due to the fact that the Democrats controlled both houses of Congress and often received support from reform-minded Republicans. Eleanor's remarks that the American people were prepared to accept anything the president advised seemed to apply to the Congress as well. From a political perspective, legislators who opposed New Deal proposals also might be forced to answer to constituents who wanted action from their government. Roosevelt also proved adept in lining up support for bills as they made their way through both House and Senate, often calling congressional leaders into the White House to explain policy and, when necessary, to apply political pressure.

The legislation of the Hundred Days blended short-term relief measures with attempts to reform the structure of the U.S. economy. As a whole, these programs and initiatives defied generalization. Some encouraged inflation and increased spending; others removed money from the economy and encouraged deflation. Some were designed to offer direct relief to the unemployed; others encouraged work through government-crafted employment projects. The diversity of this legislative tidal wave was an indication that Roosevelt was open to any ideas that might yield results. He enjoyed hearing different sides of the same issue, hoping to locate a position that made the most sense. Policy meetings with advisors often became debate sessions, with Roosevelt serving as referee and judge. He never displayed a commanding understanding of the details surrounding particular problems. Statistics seemed to bore him, and he did not trust individuals who seemed to operate with a political or ideological agenda. At times, advisors complained that Roosevelt never really seemed to comprehend the data presented to him and tended to govern based on his gut rather than on rational deliberation.

A strength he did have, however, was an ability to encourage constructive discussion within the brain trust. Taking on the role of coach, Roosevelt admonished his experts to dig deep to find solutions. At times this style of leadership was a recipe for infighting as members of the team sought to curry favor with their chief. For the most part, however, he was able to keep them on course. The respect he was able to command from this group, which included several egoistic personalities, was impressive. Retired Supreme Court Justice Oliver Wendell Holmes, Jr., upon meeting Roosevelt, remembered him as displaying a "second-class intellect—but a first-class temperament." Intellectuals who examined the presidency from the outside complained that Roosevelt was a dilettante, which was not completely unfair. Nevertheless, his leadership style did yield results.

While the banking crisis had demanded immediate attention, Roosevelt entered the presidency with the view that the condition of agriculture was the most severe problem confronting the nation. For farmers, the Depression had worsened an already bad situation. While most Americans had prospered during the Roaring Twenties, farmers had watched their incomes dwindle due to falling crop prices since the end of World War I. By 1933, grain prices had dropped to the point that many farmers saw little need to take their yield to market. Farm foreclosures had increased for years; the stock market crash and the resultant strain on credit made the problem all the worse. Increasing numbers of farmers lost their lands and, with few prospects, migrated into urban areas or ventured westward to California to find work.

Discussions over the plight of the American farmer had been taking place for years. Reformers, in fact, had sought a restructuring of the economy to address overproduction and falling prices since the Populist era of the late nineteenth century. In the 1920s, progressives in both parties had proposed a variety of means to absorb excess crops, which might drive prices upward, including government-sponsored storage systems, subsidies paid to farmers to scale back production, and increased exporting of goods. Roosevelt spent much time in the months prior to the inauguration discussing agricultural policy with Wallace and Tugwell, both of whom were committed to significant reform. The most popular idea was a subsidy program that would allow farmers to decrease the amount of acreage farmed without suffering a loss of income. Within days following the inauguration, the team drew up a set of proposals to send to Congress.

While some of the bills of the Hundred Days sped through the legislature, there was heated debate over Roosevelt's agricultural policies. Conservatives charged that federally controlled production was equivalent to socialism and rejected the idea as far too radical. Reformers, however, outnumbered these voices and passed the Farm Relief Act, a bill with several components. Most notably, the legislation called for the creation of a new government agency, the Agricultural Adjustment Administration (AAA), placed in charge of overseeing New Deal farming programs. The AAA would offer subsidies for farmers who participated by agreeing to cut back the amount of land used in cultivation. Fewer crops on the market would mean rising prices.

The AAA, headed by George Peek and placed under the watch of Henry Wallace, generated considerable criticism, even among some moderates, and turned out to be something of a public relations fiasco for the administration. In an effort to get a jump on excess supplies of cotton, other crops, and livestock, agents working for Peek encouraged farmers to destroy existing stockpiles of their commodities or to butcher their animals. Raising prices, according to economists, required proactive measures to address the glut that already existed. The policy may have made economic sense, but the sight of goods being destroyed in rural areas while the urban unemployed had trouble affording food seemed to many a ludicrous proposition. The new agency was met with disdain from all fronts. While conservatives continued to rail about its violation of free market principles, others complained that the program did little to aid those most in need—family farmers and tenant laborers. This complaint was not without merit, for AAA subsidies favored large agricultural enterprises since the funds were doled out based on acreage. Furthermore, cutting back crop production meant less need for employment on large farms, making the plight of many farm laborers even worse.

The New Deal's initial foray into farm policy yielded mixed results. The AAA did manage to curtail production, as the amount of land used for cultivation declined three-fold. Prices also began to rise, in many cases for the first time in more than a decade, and continued to increase for several years. Yet Roosevelt had spent political capital in implementing these polices, and the AAA continued to be an easy target for opponents of the New Deal. From the start, critics questioned the constitutionality of the program; soon challenges appeared in the courts. Roosevelt, undaunted, moved forward and at least could point to the fact that he had achieved real reform. For the first time in history, the federal government had taken significant steps to reverse the plight of the American farmer.

Industrial recovery presented perhaps an even greater challenge. The essential problem was the same as in agriculture—falling prices caused by a combination of overproduction and lack of income on behalf of consumers. Since the Depression began, business owners had struggled to keep prices at reasonable levels. Hoover's response to complaints of unfair price-cutting had been to encourage stability through voluntary price controls and also by imploring businesses to maintain fair practices. When some business leaders approached him with the concept of developing price levels through government coordination, Hoover responded negatively. The free market, he argued, would eventually work its way through these problems of supply and demand.

Roosevelt agreed with this sentiment. Having cut his political teeth on the progressivism of Woodrow Wilson, he carried from his wartime experience a concern about the potential power of corporate America. During his years in the Navy Department, he had learned how business owners would make a mockery of open competition by working to fix prices or monopolize government contracts. He and Josephus Daniels had followed a policy of encouraging competitive bidding, believing that competition was healthy for the economy. He also supported Wilson's New Freedom, which sought to prevent unfair consolidation of trusts and monopolies.

Yet the president's antimonopoly sentiments had their limit. The wartime experience had also shown him how coordination between government and industry could achieve efficiency and effectively check price gouging. Most of his advisors on industrial recovery were progressives in the tradition of Theodore Roosevelt's New Nationalism and approached reform in terms of regulation implemented with the support, rather than the antagonism, of big business. Tugwell in particular was influential in moving Roosevelt to the view that proactive government planning could alter the course of the economy, but only if carried out with the participation of business leaders.

The industrial recovery bill that Roosevelt sent to Congress was in many ways more ambitious than the Farm Relief Act. The National Industrial Recovery Act called on businesses to create associations responsible for formulating fair codes of conduct within an industry, particularly in the area of price structuring. The act anticipated potential negative impacts that such cooperation might have on organized labor and also included guarantees that workers would have the right to join unions that would be allowed to engage in collective bargaining. The bill's labor provisions, spelled out in Section 7(a), became historic legislation for the U.S. labor movement in that the federal government would now affirm and support the presence of labor in the economy.

Hugh Johnson, a headstrong World War I general, became head of a new agency created by the act, the National Recovery Administration (NRA), which was charged with overseeing the implementation of business codes. From the outset, Johnson expected the NRA to be an ordeal, anticipating a great deal of hostility from a business community that would bristle from these new regulations. Instead, the opposite occurred. Business owners rushed to join the NRA in search of stability and for an opportunity to create a floor for pricing within their industries. During the first few months of the NRA's existence, hundreds of business leaders flocked to Washington to participate; their work generated a system of codes for prices, wages, production schedules, and labor policy.

The administration launched the NRA with great fanfare. The president addressed the public in another fireside chat to promote the idea. A parade marched through New York City celebrating the new agency. Johnson helped to transform the program into a national crusade of sorts by developing a nationwide advertising campaign to raise awareness of the new codes. The NRA's symbol became the "Blue Eagle," and participating businesses were encouraged to display a placard on storefronts with the agency's slogan: "We Do Our Part." This appeal to patriotism yielded impressive results, because businesses found that refusal to play a role in combating the Depression could result in negative publicity. Roosevelt had compared the crisis to a war; now the NRA would serve as a vanguard through which to fight it.

Roosevelt believed industrial reform to be the most significant of the Hundred Days and believed that it would reverse the course of the economy. As with the AAA, though, the NRA quickly became the target of critics. While businesses showed enthusiasm for the codes early on, their attitude soured as prices began to creep up without a corresponding increase in profits. With wages remaining steady, and with little increase in the ability of consumers to purchase products, a small amount of price inflation in no way brought about an economic boom. Also, just as the AAA seemed to benefit large farms, the NRA tended to favor large businesses and corporations at the expense of smaller enterprises. Price controls placed a severe burden on small companies that had very small profit margins. Even organized labor was less than effusive in its praise for the program. Some labor leaders complained that Section 7(a) only served the interests of well-established unions; unorganized workers in low-wage, nonskilled jobs saw few benefits. Among the more notable opponents to the NRA was John L. Lewis, the fiery head of the United Mine Workers of America, who refused to participate. Lewis and other industrial labor leaders launched a crusade to organize industrial workers into a new organization, the Committee of Industrial Organizations. Lewis became a strong and persistent critic of the Roosevelt administration.

As months passed, the popularity of the NRA declined even more. Americans were less than enthusiastic about rising prices with no visible increases in wages. The program was launched with the hopes of encouraging national unity; instead, what critics derided as the "National Run-Around" seemed to generate more division. Roosevelt's opponents charged that the policy violated the Constitution, and, by the end of the NRA's first year, some Democrats in Congress had joined in this chorus of opposition. Roosevelt held firm to the view that, if given time, the NRA would produce visible results. As the Depression moved into its fourth, and eventually its fifth, year, however, patience began to run thin.

The final prong of Roosevelt's industrial recovery program was the development of government-sponsored work programs to combat unemployment. In this area the New Deal differed from Hoover's administration in degree rather than substance. The creation of public works projects had been a central feature of the former president's economic program as a means to help individuals to help themselves. Unlike some recovery initiatives, public works also were popular with Congress, as projects pumped money and job opportunities into specific states and districts.

Bills originated in the legislature on a regular basis requesting more funds for employment projects in all parts of the country.

During the Hundred Days, the administration announced the creation of a new Public Works Administration; Congress not only approved the plan but also requested five billion dollars, which was far more than even Roosevelt had envisioned. The new agency, under the watch of Secretary of the Interior Harold Ickes, accepted proposals for projects such as highway construction, bridges, ports, and buildings. For the results-oriented president, public works was an attractive means for recovery. Public works projects also were more attractive than direct relief, as Roosevelt agreed with Hoover that direct unemployment payments could become, as he called them, a "narcotic" that might lull people into complacency and dependence. The main problem was the cost. Massive projects required enormous spending that would strain the national budget and lead ultimately to deficits—a scenario that Roosevelt was unwilling to contemplate in the first years of his presidency.

With time, however, Roosevelt began to change his attitude regarding the dangers of deficits, which sparked an explosion of new works programs. For some time, economists in the United States had been moving to the view that increased government spending could be instrumental in fueling economic growth. The British economist John Maynard Keynes did more to popularize the use of deficit spending to promote growth; by the time Roosevelt became president this theory was becoming more accepted in academic circles. By the end of his first term in office, the administration had moved to accept Keynesian theory as part of its economic recovery program. The influx of dollars into the economy through government spending, the thinking went, might "prime the pump" of the economy and trigger expansion that eventually would overcome any short-term deficits.

With the door opened for new programs, in 1935 the administration launched a new wave of projects through the Works Progress Administration (WPA), which was far more ambitious and far-reaching than its predecessor. Originally capitalized with 10 billion dollars, the WPA promoted employment not only through the construction of infrastructure, but also in several other areas. The Federal Writers Project and the Federal Theatre Project, for example, employed thousands of writers and artists and transformed the relationship between the federal government and the arts. A National Youth Administration targeted Americans between the ages of 16 and 24 and generated over one million part-time and full-time jobs. While critics called into question this enhanced role for government, WPA projects were quite popular with the public. These programs also gave the administration even more leverage with Congress, as Roosevelt could now hold out the possibility of WPA funds in exchange for support for other initiatives. The WPA remained in place for the duration of the Depression and was among the longest-lasting recovery programs of the administration.

Another indication that Roosevelt was open to experimentation was his strong support for a rural electrification project in the valley of the Tennessee River, a massive proposal that combined public works with government control of utilities. The concept of public utilities was not new. During the Progressive Era several cities and states moved to government administration of power, plumbing, and transportation. As governor of New York, Roosevelt had promoted the development of hydroelectric power facilities on the St. Lawrence River. In the aftermath of World War I, reformers had proposed the creation of a power facility to be built on the Tennessee River at Muscle Shoals, Alabama, that would bring electricity to cities, towns, and rural areas in a large, multistate region in the mid-South—a project that met with little enthusiasm from Coolidge and Hoover. Even before the election, Roosevelt had begun to learn about the project and decided to promote it as part of the Hundred Days. The Tennessee Valley Authority (TVA) passed through Congress in April 1933, and construction on a hydroelectric dam began within months. Over the next several decades, the TVA brought power to growing numbers of households and businesses and became a permanent fixture in Tennessee, Alabama, and Georgia.

This whirlwind of activity during the first two years of the New Deal focused exclusively on the economy, as Roosevelt had promised to make the Depression the main focus of his presidency. If there was an irony here, it lay in the fact that Roosevelt always had a more keen interest in foreign policy than in domestic issues. Although they took a back seat to the economy, there were significant challenges the administration faced in the international arena. In Europe, the ascendancy of the National Socialist Workers, or Nazi Party, in Germany was particularly troublesome. Adolf Hitler, who obtained the title of chancellor exactly one day after Roosevelt was sworn in as president, rose to prominence through an explosive mixture of anti-Semitism, racial nationalism, and militarism. The Nazis immediately launched a wave of brutality against German Jews, separating them from the rest of society through a series of discriminatory laws.

While other governments in Europe were alarmed by these events, Hitler's repudiation of the Versailles Treaty that had ended World War I was even more threatening. Speeches he gave in the German parliament promised that the limitations on German industrial and military development by the victors of that war would be rescinded and that the nation would soon become a power in central Europe. Roosevelt, who referred to Hitler as a "madman," agreed with his counterparts in England and France that caution should guide their course in dealing with the traumatized nation. Disarmament talks held in Geneva, Switzerland, in 1933 resulted in an international agreement that championed peace and nonaggression; Hitler's willingness to sign the document masked serious changes taking place in Europe. For now, though, as the United States and its allies struggled to overcome the Depression, there was optimism that an international crisis could be averted through negotiation.

Circumstances in Asia were even more threatening. Relations between the United States and Japan had been strained for decades and were now approaching a crisis. In 1931, the Japanese had launched a military expedition onto the mainland with the intention of colonizing the region of Manchuria in northwest China. Hoover responded with a firm stance by refusing to recognize Japanese authority in the area and called for immediate withdrawal. Roosevelt was resolved to maintain pressure on the Japanese to end its aggressive foreign policy, even hinting of the possibilities of war in the early months of his presidency. As the Japanese military pushed further into China, Roosevelt obtained from Congress authority to impose trade sanctions, a move that met with opposition from isolationists who interpreted the action as unnecessarily antagonistic. This tension relaxed in May 1933, when Japan halted its advances and made overtures for a truce with the Chinese government. The crisis settled for the time being. However, the true intentions of the Japanese government were unclear, as its troops had pushed to within a few hundred miles of the Chinese capital of Peking.

These international stresses captured much more attention in Washington than in other parts of the country, as most Americans seemed little concerned with events abroad. As the New Deal moved into its third year, the sluggish economy continued to be the center of attention. Roosevelt could point to an impressive legislative achievement during his first two years in office and encouraged the public to allow time for recovery measures to take effect. However, patience was in short supply across the country. With unemployment levels remaining high, and with little substantial growth in economic activity, popularity for the New Deal began to wane. As Roosevelt began to contemplate plans for his reelection campaign, he found his policies besieged on all fronts.

The New Deal's twin pillars of recovery, the AAA and the NRA, both were in retreat due to dwindling expectations. Roosevelt's agricultural policy from the start had been attacked by conservatives as too radical. Now, it was receiving complaints from others as well. Farmers of modest means had seen little improvement since these reforms were implemented, and by mid-decade their plight was reaching the status of a national epic. The Dust Bowl on the Great Plains, the result of several years of unusually dry weather and overuse of land, led to increasing numbers of foreclosures and the uprooting of entire families. Mother Nature seemed to be mocking the American farmer, who had endured financial hardship for decades prior to the Depression.

The experiences of Dust Bowl migrants were popularized by writers such as John Steinbeck and served to intensify criticism of the New Deal. The problem haunted Roosevelt, who considered himself an advocate of the "yeoman farmer," and led him to seek out new avenues of reform. Tugwell, who had played a significant role in designing the AAA, explained the problem as one of organization. In his view, the days of the independent family farmer had passed, and farmers would have to enter into collective arrangements to improve cultivation and gain a stronger position in the marketplace. Operating on these assumptions, Tugwell became head of the Resettlement Administration (RA) in the spring of 1935, designed to encourage cooperative farming, including collective arrangements for purchasing machinery, setting production schedules, and coordinating sales. The most ambitious part of the plan, and the most controversial, lay in the RA's attempts to encourage farmers to sell unproductive land and move into cooperative farm areas where groups of growers would share ownership of their farms and their profits. Tugwell intended for the program to revolutionize farming by resettling as many as half a million families, a goal that required much more money than the administration or Congress was willing to donate. The RA also generated more attacks from the right, as opponents compared the program to Soviet-style collectivization of agriculture. In all, only a few thousand farmers received support for resettlement.

Even more problematic was the news that the Supreme Court had struck down the AAA on grounds that the program violated the Constitution. A case involving a textile mill in New England had found its way into the court system over a year prior to the decision. Roosevelt was prepared for a legal challenge but expected the Court to refrain from overturning his recovery policies. Instead, the Court ruled, in a six-to-three decision, that efforts to regulate production with the intent of controlling prices represented an overreach of federal authority. The decision, which frustrated Roosevelt, placed the administration's entire agricultural reform policy in limbo. The other concern was the issue of industrial recovery. If the Court had rejected the AAA, then there was every reason to expect a similar result with respect to the NRA.

Those fears were realized when the Court ruled unanimously that the NRA violated constitutional limitations on federal regulation of private industry. Invoking stern language, the Court determined that the Depression, despite its seriousness, was not a valid reason for overstepping the bounds of the commerce clause of the Constitution. Because much of the industry regulated by the NRA was contained within a single state, the Court concluded that the federal government had no authority to control prices, wages, or production levels. These two decisions left Roosevelt's entire recovery program in shambles. Despite his outrage, he avoided criticizing the Supreme Court in public. Yet the confrontation with the Court was not over. These challenges convinced Roosevelt that an overly conservative judiciary represented a roadblock to recovery. His growing mistrust of the federal bench ultimately led to a dramatic showdown in his second term.

Two years in office had yielded mixed results. Roosevelt certainly delivered on his promise for action; the problem lay in the fact that the legislative onslaught of the Hundred Days had not reversed the course of the economy. While the administration trumpeted modest gains in productivity and slight increases in employment numbers, few Americans were under the impression that the Depression had come to an end. Undaunted by attacks from both the left and the right, by 1935 Roosevelt was prepared to move forward with a new wave of reform. The final two years of the first term, which has been described by historians as the "Second New Deal," offered more structural, long-term reform in contrast to the recovery measures that marked the early New Deal. With respect to domestic issues, these two years perhaps were the most significant of his presidency.

This new wave of legislation was, in part, a response to social movements that had gained support beyond Washington. The most significant of these was led by a Florida doctor named Francis Townsend, who had launched a campaign to raise awareness for the plight of the elderly poor. His descriptions of Americans in their seventies and eighties, whose pensions had disappeared and who had no family support, generated sympathy from readers across the country. The retired physician also designed a plan, which attracted thousands of supporters into "Townsend Clubs," that provided a guaranteed monthly income to the elderly financed by new taxes on businesses. This streak of populism in Townsend's message resonated with large numbers of working-class Americans.

The concept of old-age unemployment insurance had been around for decades. Reformers, for example, often pointed out that the United States was the only industrialized nation in the Western world that did not have some sort of support system for the elderly. Yet such a program of wealth redistribution as Townsend's did not sit well with Roosevelt. From the outset of his presidency, he had engaged in conversation with Secretary of Labor Perkins about possible legislation to create a federally administered unemployment insurance system; with Townsend now drawing so much attention to the issue, Roosevelt sensed that the timing was right to submit a bill to Congress. As with much of the New Deal, the Social Security Act charted a middle course between more radical programs, such as Townsend's, and conservative views that opposed any government activity. The Social Security Administration, founded in the summer of 1935, was a watershed moment in the nation's history. While not creating a full-blown system of social welfare that some reformers had wanted, for the first time ever the federal government took on a role in promoting financial security for citizens.

The other landmark legislation signed that year was the National Labor Relations Act, sponsored by New York Senator Robert F. Wagner. The Supreme Court's overturning of the major provisions of the National Industrial Recovery Act had left the administration's labor policy in disarray. Wagner and other congressional proponents of labor reform had worked for over a year to design a new labor bill, and support for such legislation made good political sense. Membership in unions, particularly among industrial workers, had grown by leaps and bounds since 1933. Yet the upsurge in organizing activity sparked a new commitment by business owners to assert control in the workplace. The result was a year marked by a wave of strikes in industrial areas; at times these conflicts became quite violent and presented the administration with a potential crisis. Support for a new labor bill grew in the Congress and arrived on Roosevelt's desk in the summer of 1935.

The Wagner Act that Roosevelt signed was significant for labor in several ways. First, the act reaffirmed the right of workers to unionize through fair electoral processes. Business owners and management who sought to block organizing efforts through intimidation would be held in violation of the law. The bill also created a National Labor Relations Board, which received authority to arbitrate disputes between labor and management that became deadlocked. For Roosevelt, the board hearkened back to his experiences during World War I, when strikes and walkouts threatened wartime production. Labor deserved legal protection when fighting for gains in the workplace; however, strikes undercut productivity and slowed growth. Roosevelt's support of the legislation established his reputation as a supporter of organized labor.

Throughout Roosevelt's first term, Eleanor charted a new course as first lady. Although she had hinted at times before the campaign that she was not overly enthusiastic about moving into the White House, she had worked tirelessly to promote her husband. When living in the governor's mansion in Albany, Eleanor had plunged into several public commitments, hoping to use her social status to promote causes she deemed worthy. Now in Washington, she took on an active political and social agenda that departed from the traditional role of the president's wife, which historically had been to serve as hostess and companion.

Over the years, Eleanor had developed strong convictions regarding civil rights and social welfare policy. She often was more committed to these issues than Franklin. She became a consistent advocate for improving conditions and opportunities for African Americans and made headlines on many occasions by commenting on the need for reforms to combat inequalities between the races. There were several other ventures as well, including her promotion of a planned community in West Virginia designed to resettle unemployed miners and industrial workers. The town, called Arthurdale, never achieved its aims of serving as a model for other planned settlements that might offer impoverished Americans more opportunities through improved conditions. Nevertheless, it was among the more ambitious reform projects carried out during the Depression. For the most part, she stayed clear of presidential politics and avoided commenting on the New Deal in public; however, her role as an activist reshaped the image of a first lady.

The Roosevelt children, now all adults, also felt the impact of their father's fame. Their activities constantly were scrutinized by the press and at times caused some difficulty for Franklin. Elliott, the youngest son, generated a media frenzy when he divorced his wife and remarried during his father's first year in office. Unlike their experience in Albany, where the family moved freely in and out of the governor's mansion, the children also found it much more difficult to gain access to Franklin. In later years, each of them, along with Eleanor, recalled the strains the presidency placed on the family. Yet each of them also carried a deeply felt admiration for their father. As time passed, a small army of grandchildren enlarged the Roosevelt clan. Most people who knew the family personally or worked near Roosevelt remarked that his favorite moments were spent with the extended family, particularly during vacations.

The first term in Washington was both exhausting and exhaustive. If for no other reason, these years had been historic for the extraordinary amount of legislation passed to combat the Depression and restructure the economy. There were still a myriad of challenges that lay ahead. The economy continued to limp along. The Supreme Court had overturned the main components of the New Deal's recovery program. The legislation of the "Second New Deal" had yet to take root. There was a great deal of work left to be done. However, the American people would first have to decide to give Roosevelt the opportunity to continue.

Chapter 9

CHALLENGES AT HOME AND ABROAD

In September 1935, Roosevelt, accompanied by Harold Ickes and Harry Hopkins, embarked upon a transcontinental journey by train that began in Washington, D.C., and ended in California. The stated reason for the trip was to raise awareness for public works and conservation projects by visiting sites such as Boulder Dam. Yet there also was an added motivation—the trip also served as an early foray into a campaign for reelection by offering the president a chance to make contact with voters. The upcoming election, in Roosevelt's mind, would be a referendum on his first term and would be crucial in generating more momentum for the New Deal.

There were reasons for both optimism and pessimism. The Democratic party, which only a few years earlier suffered from regional and ideological rifts, seemed to be in good graces with the public. The 1934 midterm elections had strengthened their numbers in Congress, a good sign for the administration. With a stronger command in both the House of Representatives and Senate, Roosevelt was hopeful that his legislative agenda would continue to score successes. Statistics collected by party researchers indicated that the president enjoyed strong support in virtually every state. More promising data also were presented by George Gallup, whose new polling techniques offered innovative ways to measure public opinion.

Despite this encouraging news, certainly not everyone was enamored with the Roosevelt name. Attacks from conservatives were to be expected; however, voices of protest on the left had begun to increase over the past year, asserting that the New Deal was built on empty promises. The most notable of these critics was Louisiana Senator Huey P. Long, who had risen to prominence in part by bashing Roosevelt's leadership.

The demagogic Long, who had built a political empire in his home state through a radical form of populism, thundered onto the national stage with a "Share Our Wealth" movement that called for a massive redistribution of wealth. His new book outlining the scheme, *Every Man A King*, which sported a brilliant gold cover, explained that seizing income from the most wealthy Americans could guarantee all a home and monthly salary. That his book sold over one million copies and sparked hundreds of Share Our Wealth Clubs around the country indicated that widespread frustration with the economy continued to exist. By 1935, Roosevelt had become Long's primary target, as he talked about making an independent run for the presidency, if not to win, at least to divert enough votes to push the New Dealers out of power.

Long's popularity caught many political leaders, Roosevelt included, off guard. More troubling was the fact that the "Kingfish," as Long liked to call himself, was not alone in capitalizing on anti–New Deal sentiment. A Detroit-based clergyman, Charles Coughlin, also had gained notoriety for his assaults on the administration. As the "radio priest," Father Coughlin broadcast a show that originally focused on matters of faith. In the previous couple of years, though, Coughlin's show morphed into one focused on politics and economics, and each week his show drew millions of listeners from coast to coast as he railed against business tycoons, liberals, and Franklin Roosevelt as the sources of poverty in the United States. In California, a well-known literary figure, Upton Sinclair, was making waves with a radical End Poverty in California movement that also derided the New Deal for its probusiness policies. With the political climate becoming increasing volatile, nothing could be left to chance in the upcoming election. Roosevelt planned on running an energetic and combative campaign.

He also felt the need to stress his credentials as a social reformer to respond to challenges on the left. His public addresses increasingly took on a populist tone moving into the election year. In January 1936, this new emphasis displayed itself in an address to Congress where he claimed that enormous concentrations of wealth in the hands of a few threatened both economic recovery and democracy. Progressives in the Senate used the opportunity to propose legislation to create a new tax on inheritances and gifts, which Roosevelt signed into law. The Wealth Tax Act fell short of the radical income redistribution scheme advanced by Huey Long; nevertheless, it gave Roosevelt ammunition with which to combat such opponents.

The president also could count on the fact that a large number of Americans lionized him. There was an aura surrounding Roosevelt in the eyes of many people, generated perhaps by his ability to show concern for those in need. Virtually every day of his entire presidency, he received letters from supporters, sometimes numbering into the hundreds per day, thanking him for his leadership. Many letters contained detailed descriptions of people's own circumstances, as writers believed that their president would not only read each one but would to respond directly to their needs. Roosevelt's penchant for connecting with the people was his greatest political asset, and while it came naturally to him it also was cultivated and designed. The fireside chats, the photographs of Roosevelt meeting with farmers and workers, the strong rhetoric aimed at corporate greed and power—all shaped the Roosevelt image.

The administration's sensitivity to developing positive relations with the press was another factor in shaping Roosevelt's image. Prior presidents had understood that positive press coverage was important to maintaining public support; Roosevelt's staff, however, revolutionized the way the executive office interacted with the mass media. Former reporter Stephen Early, who handled press coverage, in effect, professionalized the position of press secretary. Photographers gained access to Roosevelt only on Early's terms, and reporters were screened before they conducted interviews. Early also pioneered the concept of the regularly scheduled press conference. Usually twice each week, a group of reporters were ushered into Roosevelt's office, where for half an hour the president engaged in dialogue with them. The mood of these sessions usually was upbeat and jovial. Roosevelt enjoyed the meetings; he came to know most of the reporters, often joking with them and creating a comfortable atmosphere for them. In exchange, their coverage tended to be complimentary.

Biographers of Roosevelt often have pointed to the issue of his disability as an example of the symbiosis that existed between the president and the press. The White House staff requested that reporters avoid asking questions about his physical condition or publishing photographs that would draw attention to it. Roosevelt's sensitivity on the matter made sense, given that during his campaign for governor of New York years earlier, questions about his ability to handle the job seemed to divert attention from issues. For the most part, journalists complied with the request. Very few photographs ever appeared, or even existed, that depicted him in a wheelchair or standing on crutches, despite the fact that opportunities to capture these images were plentiful. Most reporters who covered Roosevelt remembered, in later years, scenes of Roosevelt requiring assistance to stand or walk, and more than one witnessed the president falling down. Few of these scenes, however, ever became public knowledge.

Hence Roosevelt entered the election with guarded optimism. Always eager for a campaign, he began consulting with advisors a year in advance to chart out a course for reelection. There was one conspicuous absence from the team, however, for Louis Howe, who had served Roosevelt loyally since his first campaign 25 years earlier, died in April 1936. His passing was not unexpected, as he had been in poor health for several years and had spent the last months of his life confined to a bed at the Bethesda Naval Hospital. To the end, Howe had worked to advance Roosevelt's career. He demanded a phone line be connected from his hospital room to the Oval Office, and called Roosevelt so often that the staff was forced at times to screen his calls. The entire family mourned the loss of this slight, bedraggled, and nervous man, who had in the beginning generated mistrust and skepticism from Eleanor and the children. His unyielding loyalty to Franklin moved them all, and he gradually was welcomed as part of the family. And while Howe's influence had faded somewhat in the past few years, his presence always had provided Roosevelt with much-needed stability. From a political standpoint, clearly he would be missed.

As the campaign shifted into high gear, the challenges posed by Long, Sinclair, Coughlin, and others became evident. The Democratic party's platform held few surprises, focusing mostly on the accomplishments of the first term and promising renewed efforts at recovery. However, Roosevelt's stump speeches contrasted considerably with those of the first presidential campaign. His first major address of the contest, delivered at Philadelphia's Franklin Field, attacked the unbridled power of "economic royalists" who sought privileges from government and squeezed out the needs of average Americans. The speech, delivered to almost 100,000 onlookers, drew thunderous applause as he generated new headline material. "To some generations, much is given," he admonished the crowd. "Of other generations much is expected. This generation has a rendezvous with destiny."

The Republican party, still reeling from the previous election, was committed to separating itself from the image of Herbert Hoover. Delegates nominated Kansas governor Alfred "Alf" Landon for the presidency at their Cleveland, Ohio, convention. Landon was a good choice. As Roosevelt had in 1928, Landon won a state election in 1932 amidst a freefall for his party in most other parts of the country. The midwesterner, who had a background in the progressive wing of his party, also had few ties to Hoover. His running mate, Chicago newspaper publisher Frank Knox, also traced his roots to Theodore Roosevelt and the "Bull Moosers" and had a strong record on foreign policy. He had, in fact, supported Franklin's efforts to strengthen the navy in the years prior to World War I.

Landon's campaign strategy was in stark contrast to Roosevelt's. He lacked his opponent's speaking skills and charisma and was not fond of campaigning. Furthermore, the Republicans had to accept Roosevelt's popularity and the widespread support the New Deal enjoyed. Rather than attacking the administration head-on, which perhaps would have yielded few dividends, Landon tried to find ways of criticizing the implementation of New Deal policies rather than the philosophy behind them. Conservatives in the party condemned what they called "me-too Republicanism" and rejected the strategy as defeatist. Roosevelt, on the other hand, capitalized on the fact that Americans had little knowledge of Landon and worked to equate the Kansan's name with Hoover. Going on the offensive, the president often described the 1920s as a time of recklessness in Washington and warned that a Republican victory would reverse the course of recovery.

The outcome of the election confirmed not only Roosevelt's popularity, but also that a reordering of the political landscape had occurred over the past four years. While most forecasters predicted his reelection, few could have anticipated the breadth of the victory. Roosevelt carried all but two states; even Landon's home state of Kansas went for the president. Democrats performed well in every part of the country, as their already-large majorities in Congress grew. In the Senate, Roosevelt's party now held a lead of 75 seats to 25. Moreover, support for the New Deal had generated significant changes in the composition of the electorate. The most stunning change came within the African American community, which until the Depression tended to support the "party of Lincoln." For the first time in history, the majority of black voters sided with the Democrats and would in the future become solid in their support for the party. Political observers, in fact, began to speak of a "Roosevelt coalition," with time became the core of the Democratic party and that included labor, ethnic, and racial minorities, along with academics and intellectuals.

Emboldened by the size of the victory, Roosevelt prepared to reenergize the New Deal by expanding it into new areas over the course of the second term. In the inaugural address, he charted an ambitious course. "I see one-third of a nation ill-housed, ill-clad, and ill-nourished," he announced. "It is not in despair that I paint you that picture. I paint it for you in hope—because the nation, seeing and understanding the injustice of it, propose to paint it out." The weather that January afternoon was dismal, as a biting cold rain pierced the crowd of onlookers. The scene was fitting, for, despite the mood of optimism that surrounded the speech, the next four years would be marked by a series of setbacks, challenges, and miscalculations for the administration.

The first significant act of Roosevelt's second term was an ill-fated collision with the Supreme Court. He had held a strong grudge against the Court since it had overturned New Deal agricultural and industrial policies a year earlier. As he saw it, the problem was not the entire bench, but rather the handful of conservative justices who blocked reform. It was inconceivable, in his view, that the actions of this group of men trumped not only the White House, but also the Congress and, presumably, the will of the people. As he mulled over their rulings, he convinced himself that this was not an issue of constitutionalism, but rather one of democracy. The question was how to overstep their assault on the New Deal and place his recovery program back on track.

For months, he searched for solutions and eventually concluded that the problem lay in the fact that several elderly justices continued to cling to their seats on the Court despite being well above retirement age. Upon entering the presidency four years earlier, Roosevelt had expected the opportunity to replace one or more members; however, the conservative block had held out for four years and managed to thwart the main tenets of the New Deal. He discussed the matter with legal experts and advisors within the administration. One suggestion was to propose an amendment to the Constitution that would call for more than a simple majority on the Court to overturn a bill passed by Congress. The plan was attractive in that it offered a means of strengthening the role of the legislative and executive branches of government, but it did so within the framework of constitutional procedures.

Yet an effort to change the Constitution would not only be difficult to achieve but also might take a great deal of time. Roosevelt ultimately abandoned the idea and instead became intrigued by Attorney General Homer Cummings's proposal that the president simply alter the number of justices sitting on the Court. This could be explained, according to Cummings, on grounds of efficiency. Roosevelt could claim that the Court, burdened by the ages of its senior members, needed an infusion of youth, which could be achieved by appointing a new member for every judge over the age of 70, of which there were six. The idea was not altogether new. Cummings in fact had discovered that Woodrow Wilson's attorney general, James C. McReynolds, had drawn up a similar plan years ago to address the number of elderly federal judges across the country. Ironically, McReynolds was now one of the justices of the Supreme Court targeted by the administration.

Initially Roosevelt was thrilled with the plan. There was nothing explicit in the Constitution regarding the size of the Court—the number nine had grown out of tradition. There had been cases in the past where presidents had altered the size of the Court, at times for blatantly political purposes. Roosevelt convinced himself that tampering with the Court on the basis of efficiency would be accepted by the public.

The argument was a weak one. Not only did the proposal unjustly question the abilities of the senior members of the Supreme Court; it also was quite clear that Roosevelt's real motivations were political—an effort to "pack" the Court with justices more supportive of New Deal reform. The entire incident was carried out in secrecy. Roosevelt and Cummings drew up the plan and sprang the Judicial Reform Act onto an unsuspecting Congress without consultation with other close advisors. Stephen Early only discovered the scheme when Roosevelt invited a group of congressional leaders to the White House in early February, where he outlined the proposal and watched the stunned and bewildered group of legislators file out of the Cabinet room afterward.

Not surprisingly, the bill generated a firestorm in Congress. Roosevelt expected support for his crusade from fellow Democrats in both houses. Instead, the proposal polarized the party. While a handful of loyalists signed on, a surprising number opposed it from the start, including many liberals who had been consistent backers of the New Deal, who may have agreed with the administration's reform agenda but viewed court packing as little more than a power-grab. A strange coalition of Republicans and progressive Democrats aligned to oppose the plan, signifying that a quick victory was doubtful. A fierce debate ensued for several weeks.

The reaction from the Supreme Court was predictable. Roosevelt knew that the conservative members of the Court, the so-called Four Horseman—Pierce Butler, George Sutherland, William Van Devanter, and James McReynolds—would be outraged. Yet for reasons unexplained, he fully expected the progressive-minded justices on the bench to back him, despite the fact that two of them were over the age of 70. In late March, as the bill languished in Congress, Chief Justice Charles Evans Hughes issued a seven-page response to the plan defending the Court against charges of being unable to do its job. The memorandum, which also was signed by progressive justice Louis Brandeis and the conservative Van Devanter as a show of solidarity, suggested that the Judicial Reform Act would compromise the cherished principle of "separation of powers." This unorthodox move by the Court to intervene in the matter was a severe setback for Roosevelt.

As debate moved into its third month, criticism mounted, and Roosevelt would have been well-advised to drop the matter altogether. Newspaper editorials assailed the plan; opponents began to use the term "dictator" to describe him. Walter Lippmann, the highly regarded intellectual who never had been fond of the president, referred to the incident as a "bloodless coup." Roosevelt remained intransigent, and, despite pleas by some of his advisors, he continued the crusade. In early March, he defended his position in a fireside chat, claiming that "we cannot yield our constitutional destiny to the personal judgment of a few men." On this occasion, however, his attempt to appeal directly to the people faltered. The Supreme Court carried with it an image of impartiality, and while many Americans supported Roosevelt's policies, the action seemed to violate the most fundamental ideals of the U.S. government.

The controversy ended at an impasse. Roosevelt, who held out for months and refused to compromise on the matter, in July finally came to accept the bill's demise and directed his allies in Congress to allow it to die. Yet Roosevelt came away from the battle feeling victorious. In late March, as Congress waged war over the bill, the Supreme Court seemingly reversed its course by upholding a minimum wage provision that two years earlier had been ruled unconstitutional. The change came from Justice Owen Roberts, a moderate who at times supported New Deal policies but also sided with the conservatives on other issues, who came down in support of the administration's case. Conspiratorial minds suggested that the change was a calculated "switch in time to save nine"—a move to placate Roosevelt. More significantly, over the next several weeks, the Court ruled in favor of other New Deal policies, including cases challenging the National Labor Relations Act and the Social Security Act. Roosevelt also received news that Justice Van Devanter had announced his plans to retire, potentially breaking the logjam that had been the source of frustration.

In later years, Roosevelt asserted that the court-packing fiasco was one in which he lost the battle but won the war—a fairly accurate assessment. Over the next few years, the composition of the Court changed significantly, as three more justices retired and were replaced with Roosevelt appointees. The administration may have prevailed, but the costs were high. In the wake of the congressional battle, he never enjoyed the solid support of the party to which he had grown accustomed. Conservative Democrats seemed emboldened by the affair; for the remainder of Roosevelt's presidency they were more willing to oppose the administration openly. With fissures emerging in the party, the momentum of the early New Deal never returned.

Just as the court-packing ordeal reached a conclusion, Roosevelt launched another political circus by attempting to oust political opponents in the Democratic party, the so-called "purge." There was concern that conservative party members, particularly in the South, now energized by their tussle with the president regarding the Supreme Court, might ultimately polarize the party and thwart further progress for the New Deal. Roosevelt believed he could draw upon his immense public appeal to boost progressive candidates running in local primary elections. As nominal head of the party, he viewed it as his duty to set its agenda and place insurgents on the defensive.

The decision to wage war against members of his own party seemed to be a departure from the political realism that had characterized his entire career. A few biographers have suggested that the purge, along with the court-packing incident, might be explained by the absence of Louis Howe's cautious voice in the White House. Regardless of the reasons for them, these strategies carried political risks that he had avoided in the past. In both cases, Roosevelt seemed to be motivated by a conviction that he was engaged in battle on behalf of the people against forces of reaction.

The purge began in earnest in the summer of 1938, when Roosevelt embarked on a series of trips to states where he would stump on behalf of pro-reform candidates. Among the early destinations was Kentucky, where he rallied support for incumbent Senator Alben W. Barkley, who was embroiled in a race for reelection against Governor A. B. "Happy" Chandler. In Georgia, he spoke on behalf of Lawrence Camp, a lawyer running against conservative Democrat Walter George for Senate nomination. In South Carolina, he stood alongside Governor Olin D. Johnson, who was attempting to oust the popular Senator "Cotton Ed" Smith. Roosevelt logged hundreds of miles hoping to influence local elections.

Despite Roosevelt's popularity, and also despite his fondness for campaigns, the purge attempt was a failure. Not only was he unable to influence the elections, but in many cases his presence triggered a backlash against what local voters viewed as an attempt to undermine local autonomy. In a few cases, Roosevelt actually may have hurt his preferred candidate's chances of victory, and if the Democrats had been divided before the purge began, by the end of the summer these fissures were even greater.

Good news seemed in short supply that year. The already-weakened party experienced significant setbacks in the midterm elections held in November. For the first time since the Hoover administration, Republicans made gains in Congress, reclaiming 81 seats in the House of Representatives and 8 in the Senate. More troubling may have been the fact that a number of noted progressive governors lost their bids for reelection.

The New Deal had reached an impasse. The mood in the White House was uncharacteristically glum.

In the midst of these setbacks, international events began to take on greater importance, and, although no one knew it at the time, over the next several years foreign affairs would push the New Deal into relative obscurity. Roosevelt had not ignored foreign policy in the first term, but economic recovery and domestic reform were his primary focus. The foreign policy team that he had assembled had, over the past few years, continued to monitor increasingly troublesome news in other parts of the world. Cordell Hull, the secretary of state, sought to create a foreign policy in line with the mood of Depression-era America.

That mood was one of isolationism. The economic crisis that had gripped the country now for almost a decade fed apathy toward events abroad. In this climate, isolationist-minded political figures held sway, and the overarching philosophy of the government was that of clearly articulated neutrality. In 1935, Congress approved a bill that restricted trade with nations engaged in war. The Neutrality Acts were triggered in part by a Senate committee led by Gerald P. Nye of North Dakota that investigated the nation's entry into World War I. The committee's report, which was something of an isolationist manifesto, concluded that the United States had been dragged into the conflict because of trade entanglements with European belligerents. The report heaped criticism on munitions manufacturers, so-called merchants of death, that had beaten the drums of war and had driven the country into the conflict.

The administration's foreign policy did little to challenge these views and often contributed to them. Part of Roosevelt's approach was rooted in political calculation. With the New Deal enjoying strong support, there was little reason to swim against the stream of public opinion. He also agreed in principle with some of these sentiments. In August 1936, Roosevelt affirmed his commitment to U.S. neutrality in a speech delivered at Chautauqua, New York. As the presidential election was just kicking into gear, he sought to make clear that the United States would continue to carry out an inward-looking foreign policy, stating that political leaders had a responsibility to stand up to those "who selfishly or unwisely would let us go to war."

As the international scene became more volatile, this cautious climate began to hinder Roosevelt's efforts to respond and gradually pushed the administration away from the isolationists. The most pressing matter may have been in Asia, where the Japanese military had launched a new wave of invasions onto the Chinese mainland in the summer of 1937 with the goal of taking territory beyond that which it claimed only a few years earlier. More troubling was the fact that the Japanese government had changed course and now talked of a greater empire throughout Asia. This island nation, with a large population but few natural resources, seemed bent on becoming a colonial power. As Japanese troops continued their assaults, the Chinese government, already weak from a civil war, lay in peril. News of atrocities committed by Japanese troops as they overran the city of Nanjing sparked even greater concern.

Roosevelt pondered his options for responding to the Asian crisis. If the Japanese conquest of China took place without resistance, military commanders there might be encouraged to press for more territory and threaten crucial U.S. locations in the Pacific, such as the Philippines. From the start, however, the national mood was a political challenge. Isolationists, concerned that a strong response might lead to war, called immediately for the president to invoke the Neutrality Acts, which would guarantee that the United States would not interfere in the Sino-Japanese War. Roosevelt, however, believed that complete withdrawal from the conflict would set a terrible precedent not only for Japan, but for the rest of the world. Furthermore, he believed that the collapse of the government in China could be disastrous for stability throughout the Pacific Rim. His first response was to implement an embargo on sales of U.S. goods to Japan as a means of protest. When isolationists in Congress learned of these intentions, they quickly accused Roosevelt of seeking to push the country toward war.

For weeks Roosevelt pondered how to sidestep neutrality without triggering a backlash. In the end, he opted for a "quarantine" of Japan, designed to express U.S. opposition to the invasion. Although a few critics pressed him to explain the difference between an embargo and a quarantine, the expected upheaval never materialized. The lack of a response may have been due to Roosevelt's adept maneuvering; Americans may have accepted the distinction. A more likely explanation was that the administration was the beneficiary of public apathy with events taking place so far from home. Either way, the quarantine did little to alter the course of things in Asia, for in following months the situation became even more desperate as the Chinese government tried to hold out against a vastly superior military. In January 1938, Roosevelt tried to bring international pressure to bear on the Japanese by sending a delegation to a League of Nations conference in Brussels to obtain a statement of opposition from the attending countries. Norman Davis, the head of the U.S. group, was somewhat limited in his options, because Roosevelt had given him specific instructions to avoid proposing any sanctions or punishments against Japan that might generate outrage in Congress. Yet the other representatives in Brussels were not interested in entering the fray either. Following the lead of the United States, the British and French also refused to take a strong stance against Japan. In the end, the conference may have done more harm, for the silence emanating from Belgium may have been received in Tokyo as encouragement to continue its expansionist policies without fear of reprisal.

Relations between the United States and Japan had become even more strained due to the sinking of a U.S. gunboat, the U.S.S. *Panay,* which was docked off the Chinese coast. For a few tense days, Roosevelt believed that war might be imminent. However, skillful diplomacy on behalf of the Japanese government averted the crisis, as a strong apology arrived in Washington with an offer to compensate for damages. By this time, Roosevelt evidently had come to the view that a confrontation with the Japanese was inevitable. However, for the time being, the only real course of action was to wait. One notable change in the administration's defense policy, in response to the *Panay* incident, was Roosevelt's request for increased funding for naval development in the Pacific, which he received from Congress in early 1938.

If possible, circumstances in Europe were even more ominous. The fascist regimes of Benito Mussolini in Italy and Adolf Hitler in Germany had built governments and economies based on militarism and were now generating a wave of fear across the continent of Europe. A brutal civil war in Spain resulted in the rise of another dictator. In March 1938, Hitler capitalized on a rising tide of extremism by announcing the annexation of Austria. The sight of Nazi troops marching triumphantly through streets of Vienna left other European leaders bewildered. The German führer explained the move by appealing to nationalism: the union sought to unify peoples of Germanic descent into a single political entity. He assured the world that he had no designs to extend the German border further, despite his oft-repeated descriptions of a powerful German Empire, or Reich. For the time being, other Europeans would take him at his word. Americans had little opinion in the matter, if public response could be measured by the amount of discussion in the press.

Germany's aggressive foreign policy, however, was only in its infancy. In the weeks following the absorption of Austria, Hitler began to suggest that more moves would be forthcoming. The next target was the Sudetenland, the eastern strip of mountainous country that had been declared part of Czechoslovakia in the aftermath of World War I. Soon German tanks and troops were pouring over the border; the helpless government in Prague pleaded futilely for assistance from the outside world. Nothing now lay between the Czech capital and the German military other than serene farmland.

Hitler's motivations and intentions were difficult to ascertain. He continued to assert that his actions essentially were defensive and rooted in national unification. The Sudetenland, although formally part of Czechoslovakia, contained a large number of German-speaking people, and Hitler maintained that the action was an attempt to rectify mistakes made at Versailles in 1919 by bringing Germans into the national fold. Seeking to avoid a catastrophe, British and French leaders traveled to Munich to consult with the führer with the aim of negotiating a settlement and preventing war. Of course, the crucial question was whether these governments were prepared to block Hitler if he moved further into Czech territory. While the world watched and anticipated a showdown, British Prime Minister Neville Chamberlain returned to London relieved that negotiations had staved off a crisis. Hitler offered assurances that he had no intentions of conquering another nation and signed an agreement to that effect. Europeans everywhere released a sigh of relief; Chamberlain stated triumphantly that "peace in our time" had prevailed.

In the White House, Roosevelt prepared for the possibilities of a wider European war while awaiting news from Munich. He had every reason to believe that Chamberlain, along with French Premier Edouard Daladier, would draw a line in the sand for Hitler and began to discuss how to assist the allies in case of conflict. He too received the news from Munich with cheer and accepted Hitler's promises that his forces would not move toward Prague. In his view, a German invasion of Czechoslovakia made little sense, considering that Hitler not only faced opposition from Britain and France, but also could count on reaction from the Soviet Union —an ally of the Czechs and certainly no friend to the Nazis. Delighted with the settlement, Roosevelt cabled all parties to offer his congratulations and approval.

While a German assault of Czechoslovakia may not have stood the test of reason, little indicated that reason guided the German state. Within days of signing the Munich Pact, Germany erupted in a wave of violence aimed at its Jewish population. On the night of November 10, 1938, Nazi thugs destroyed Jewish-owned businesses and storefronts in cities across the country, burned down more than one hundred synagogues, and placed thousands of Jewish citizens in concentration camps. This *Kristallnacht*, or "Night of the Broken Glass," was the horrific culmination of years of persecution against German Jews promoted and carried out by the Nazis. Roosevelt was visibly shaken and expressed his outrage publicly by recalling the United States ambassador. While the tragedy touched some Americans, most considered that matter of little consequence and certainly did not read it as a precursor to war.

These events did, however, prompt Roosevelt to begin a reevaluation of defense strategy. Aware of the isolationist orientation of Congress, he nevertheless intended to place the nation on the ready in the event of a war in Europe. Privately he revealed his suspicions that Hitler's rhetoric of peace masked more sinister dreams of dominating the continent. Yet charting a new course would require much political finesse.

In early 1939, Roosevelt sought to relax limitations placed on the administration due to the Neutrality Acts. Under current law, should England and France be forced into war against Hitler, the United States would be hindered from offering any assistance. His January state of the union address indicated the change in his thinking and stood in stark contrast to earlier speeches that said little regarding international events. Now, foreign policy was at center stage, and Roosevelt declared that a policy of neutrality in the face of danger would result in disaster. In the days and weeks that followed, he worked to gain support for a significant reworking of the legislation. If nothing else, the laws as they stood encouraged Hitler to continue his reckless policies, because the United States was committed to staying out of the fray.

In mid-March, Hitler made a mockery of the Munich agreement by plunging his troops into the heart of Czechoslovakia. Now all pretenses of Hitler's policies being driven by nationalist impulse were eradicated. The führer's ultimate aim now seemed to be the port city of Danzig on the Baltic Sea, a German-speaking city that had been placed under international supervision in 1919. To get there, Hitler's forces would have to go through Poland. In the meantime, Germany's ally Italy sent troops across the Adriatic Sea and occupied Albania in the Balkans. Britain and France reeled.

The invasion of Czechoslovakia assured Roosevelt that a wider European war was imminent. This realization did not, however, result in immediate changes in policy. He refused to recognize German control of Czech territory and announced that tariff rates on German exports would be increased as retaliation. For the time being, this would have to be adequate. Efforts behind the scenes to line up support for a revision of the Neutrality Acts seemed to be making some headway as events in Europe grew more threatening. Yet he also knew that the votes were not there and that he would have to wait it out. In the interim, the Roosevelts hosted King George VI and Queen Elizabeth of England at the White House. The visit had been arranged a year earlier, but the timing was excellent in that it affirmed ties between the two countries. Private discussions with the king revealed the mood of desperation that pervaded the British government.

The next domino fell in August, when Soviet Premier Joseph Stalin announced to a shocked Western world that he had signed a nonaggression pact with Hitler. The agreement between these historic rivals caught everyone off guard and set even more shockwaves across Europe. To this point, German expansion theoretically had been checked by the fact that the Russians would oppose encroachments into Eastern Europe. This threat, combined with diplomatic pressure from the West, offered some confidence of keeping the Nazis under some control. Stalin, the steely autocrat who had in previous years launched a campaign of terror within his own country, had made the move in anticipation of Hitler's invasion of Poland and hoped to make the best of the situation by seizing territory in Eastern Europe himself. The Nazi-Soviet Pact gave the German military a green light to further its plans of conquest.

It was three o'clock in the morning of September 1 when Roosevelt was awakened by a phone call from William Bullitt, the United States ambassador to France. The transatlantic line made Bullitt's words difficult to hear, and he was soon cut off, but Roosevelt understood the message. German troops had moved into Poland. Presumably, Britain and France had already issued war declarations, a fact confirmed over the next several hours. Only two decades had passed since the European world had been ripped to shreds by World War I, the conflict described as the "war to end all wars." Now the continent would be drenched with blood again.

As the Nazi war machine raged through Poland, Roosevelt attempted to place the United States on a war footing while continuing to declare intentions to stay out of the conflict. In a fireside chat delivered on September 3, he assured listeners that no plans were underway to abandon the policy of neutrality. "I hope the United States will stay out of this war," he noted. "As long as it remains within my power to prevent, there will be no blackout of peace." Yet he also had no plans of equating neutrality with impartiality, and he fully expected and encouraged Americans to support, at least in spirit, the Allied cause. As he saw it, "even a neutral cannot be asked to close his mind or his conscience."

The speed with which Hitler's blitzkrieg, or "lightening war," cut through Poland only fueled panic. France and Great Britain, facing the massive military machine that Hitler had assembled in Germany for several years, sorely were in need of defense assistance. Roosevelt hoped to supply them with as much weaponry and materiel as possible, but there were impediments. First, the problem of the Neutrality Acts still lingered. On September 21, he delivered an emotional speech to a joint session of Congress, where he voiced not only his opposition to the laws, but regret for signing them in the first place. Yet even now, he understood that militant language might set off a wave of isolationist opposition and undermine the support he had managed to gain. He assured his audience that the course of action would be limited to "cash-and-carry" arrangements with Britain and France, meaning that American vessels would not be permitted to sail into belligerent waters loaded with weapons or other goods.

Response to Roosevelt's proposal was mixed. While public opinion clearly sided with the Allies, there was strong support for neutrality. Critics of the administration warned that Roosevelt's assurances of neutrality were a ruse and masked his real intentions of moving the country into the war. After several weeks of deliberation, Congress approved the cash-and-carry policy, a decision met with great relief in the White House. Much-needed resources could now be sold to those armies pitted against Hitler.

Cash-and-carry provisions did not, however, solve the question of the degree of military support the United States could afford to offer without compromising the nation's own defenses. While the Allies welcomed the opportunity to purchase guns, ammunition, parts, and other goods, their needs were far greater. Warplanes, tanks, and destroyers would be necessary to defeat Germany and Italy. Roosevelt found himself tiptoeing around a sensitive set of issues. While committed to seeing Hitler defeated, as commander-in-chief he also had to consider the possibility that Germany would prevail in Europe. If it did, Americans would need a strong defense to protect the nation. Military officials explained to Roosevelt that naval defenses in both the Atlantic and Pacific were weak. Defense appropriations would have to be approved by Congress before significant increases could occur, which would take time. And even with more funds at the military's disposal, a significant build-up would take months, perhaps years.

Events occurring over the next few months indicated that time was not something the United States could count on. In late November, a new crisis erupted when the Soviet Union launched an invasion of Finland. Stalin evidently feared that Hitler would violate the nonaggression agreement made only months earlier and eventually would become an adversary. The acquisition of Finland would supply the Soviets with more ports and also serve as a buffer between Germany and the U.S.S.R. The besieged Finnish government immediately turned to the United States for assistance, but Roosevelt had little to offer. Americans looked on while the helpless Finns valiantly fought for their homeland against a vastly superior force. This act of Soviet aggression served to reinforce Roosevelt's view that national defenses had to be strengthened in a timely manner. In his January 1940 state of the union address, he heaped ridicule on those who opposed a defense buildup and increased involvement in the European war as "American ostriches" who buried their heads in the sand in the face of danger.

A winter lull that had occurred following the fall of Poland ended abruptly in April 1940, when the German blitzkrieg again sprang into action. The first targets were Denmark and Norway, which both fell in a matter of days. In May, the Nazis launched the largest offensive in the war to date. Hitler began the war convinced that the strategy deployed by the Germans in World War I had been sound in theory but poor in execution. In order to stabilize the Western front, an attack would occur into France through neutral Belgium, which would result in an end-run around the bulk of French forces assembled at the German border. This renewal of the Schlieffen plan began in earnest on May 10, as troops, tanks, and planes barreled through the Netherlands, Belgium, and Luxembourg. Only six days later, the Germans had reached the French border.

As they had in World War I, the French defenses would have to hold. The news that filtered in from Europe, however, was discouraging. With modern military technology, the Germans sliced through French installations with seeming ease. By the end of May, combined French, British, and Belgian troops found themselves pinned up against the English Channel. England's new prime minister, the battle-hardened former commander Winston Churchill, updated the White House regularly but had little to offer in the way of optimism. France teetered on the brink, and a report that the British were evacuating troops from the continent signified that the end was near. The French government held out for only a few weeks more before signing an armistice on June 22. Now England faced Hitler alone.

The war had reached a pivotal moment. In the days prior to the fall of France, Maréchal Pétain, now in charge of the collapsing French government, issued a plea that the United States declare war on Germany. Roosevelt considered the possibility but was aware that there was little support in Congress or across the country for U.S. intervention. For the first time, frank discussions were taking place regarding a plan of action should Hitler win the war. In the White House, Roosevelt juggled these challenges with another set of questions. He rapidly was approaching the end of his second term as president, and he had decisions to make regarding both the future of his own career and that of the nation.

Chapter 10

A WAR PRESIDENT

Roosevelt was not the first president in the nation's history to consider breaking with tradition and running for a third term. As recently as 1920, Woodrow Wilson, embroiled in debate over U.S. entry into the League of Nations, had suggested to those close to him that he might do so but decided against it because of health problems and fear of negative reaction from within the party. Roosevelt actually had been contemplating another campaign as early 1937; in fact, in the weeks following his election to a second term, speculation emerged that he might be a three-term president due simply to the wide margin of his victory. Serious discussion on the matter began following the outbreak of war in Europe.

Democratic leaders had to face the stark reality that the entire party, to a large degree, had become personified by Roosevelt and that his absence from the 1940 campaign might leave them in disarray. For over a year leading up to the election, a number of political figures made inquiries seeking to discover whether the president would indeed be interested in reelection. While the discussions, and at times gossiping, continued, Roosevelt remained silent. Perhaps to his delight, reticence only fueled more speculation as to what his future held. The president, always a fan of poker, enjoyed the bluffing game a great deal.

Yet beneath the bluff was strong evidence that Roosevelt really was ambivalent. He was confident enough in winning the nomination from the party and knew that he would be the favorite in the election. There also were legitimate reasons to step down from office. On at least one occasion, he indicated a concern that the party had become too dependent on him, which weakened the party nationwide. This sentiment, clearly fallout from the purge fiasco, encouraged him to bow out for the health of the party. Another, and probably more pressing, matter was the question of public reaction. The previous term had not been without its challenges, and there was the very real possibility that voters would be cold to the decision. Even as the Democrats began organizing their convention, held in Chicago, few knew where he stood. Even the family was in the dark. Eleanor knew he was struggling with the question; she and many others took note when he began discussing possible employment in the private sector in early 1940.

Historians disagree about whether this period of mystery was calculated to determine public opinion on a third term or whether it simply was a case of indecision. Probably both were at work. By the time the convention began, however, there were clear signs that he intended to run again. Most of the delegates fully expected Roosevelt to win the nomination, but the party also sought to avoid making the event seem like a coronation rather than a selection. Senator Alben Barkley of Kentucky began the gamesmanship in his keynote address, where he assured the delegates that they were free to select anyone they desired. What followed, perhaps orchestrated, were chants of "We Want Roosevelt" and "America Wants Roosevelt" that echoed through the hall. The president won the nomination by a huge margin on the first ballot.

If his actions prior to the convention had been hampered by indecision, once Roosevelt received the nomination he made it clear that he intended to control the ticket. He planned to replace Vice President John Nance Garner of Texas, a conservative who had openly criticized the bid for another term. Had Louis Howe still been alive, he no doubt would have advised Roosevelt to select someone outside the inner circle, and preferably a moderate, as his running mate. Instead, Roosevelt decided that Henry Wallace, the idealistic progressive from the Midwest who had been a major player in the administration, should be Garner's successor. The selection outraged a large number of delegates, many of whom had shared Garner's opposition to Roosevelt but decided against an open fight on the convention floor. As these insurgents prepared to block Wallace, Roosevelt went on the offensive by threatening to drop out of the race if the party selected someone other than his choice. He angrily began drafting a letter of resignation from the White House while the convention stumbled forward. In the end, Roosevelt had his way, as Wallace won narrowly. The acrimony sparked by the selection of Wallace was such that the new running mate elected to forego an acceptance speech.

These open divisions within the Democratic party hearkened back to the dark years of the 1920s, and the Republicans who came together in Philadelphia for their own convention hoped to make the most of it. Their nominee for president, Wendell Willkie, was something of a surprise. The former Indianan, who had made a fortune on Wall Street in the utilities business, had been a Democrat for much of his life; as recently as 1932 he had voted for Roosevelt. Since then, however, he had become a vocal critic of the New Deal. Although a relative unknown in politics, Willkie proved a formidable candidate. His slightly unkempt appearance gave him a look of innocence in contrast to the refined Roosevelt. He also cultivated a fiery stage presence as he railed passionately against the administration.

The 1940 campaign turned out to be more caustic in tone than Roosevelt's earlier contests. Willkie was sensitive to the popularity of the New Deal and hoped instead to tap into isolationist sentiments by focusing on foreign policy. His strategy was to brand Roosevelt as an erratic interventionist who already had designs on taking the nation to war. He warned that a vote for Roosevelt would result in parents sending their sons off to die in a far-away conflict. At the same time, he displayed nuance by indicating strong support for Great Britain and supported the administration's decision to send destroyers to England in exchange for leases on naval bases previously held by the British. In response, Roosevelt offered his own brand of campaign rhetoric by declaring that the Republicans, if they gained the White House, would dismantle the New Deal and in the process destroy American democracy. More than once, the president used the term "dictator" to describe his challenger.

The campaign may have been Roosevelt's most challenging. In the midst of a volatile political atmosphere, he continued to respond to events in Europe. He had carried out the "destroyers-for-bases" deal with the understanding that it might invite criticism from isolationists. More notably, he took on the issue of military conscription at the peak of the campaign season rather than waiting until after the election. Since the war began, he had hoped to implement a draft registration system to aid in defense preparedness. After months of discussion, a plan emerged in late summer that could be sent to Congress for approval. Some of Roosevelt's advisors suggested that moving forward would prove disastrous to the campaign, for it played directly into Willkie's strategy. Roosevelt's response was that waiting until after the election would seem overtly political. He did proceed cautiously, however, by allowing Democrats in Congress to maneuver the bill and to avoid drawing public attention to it. For his part,

Willkie actually supported registration, which forced him into silence on the matter at the risk of looking hypocritical. Roosevelt signed a Selective Service Act in September that required all men aged 21 to 45 to register and make themselves eligible for a draft.

In the end, voters made clear their desire for Roosevelt's return. While the margin of victory was less than in the previous two elections, he nonetheless garnered an impressive 55 percent of the popular vote and won overwhelmingly in the Electoral College, 449 to 82. Roosevelt's critics, however, continued to speak out against the third term, sparking a movement to place a limit on the office. Congress eventually passed a bill, in 1947, allowing for a constitutional amendment to establish a two-term limit, which was ratified as the Twenty-Second Amendment four years later.

With the election behind him, Roosevelt could now operate without the air of politics lingering with every decision. Exhausted from the campaign, he left for a Caribbean cruise a few days later that was designed for relaxation but also became a working vacation. While onboard, he read a letter from Winston Churchill explaining the dire situation with respect to British defenses. The policy of cash and carry was reaching its limit, as the government in London was running low on funds to purchase U.S. munitions. When Roosevelt returned to Washington on December 17, now somewhat rejuvenated, he announced a new plan, formulated while on the open seas: the United States could offer the Allies hardware on a "lend-lease" basis. He explained the idea, which evidently was his own, to reporters by using an analogy of a neighbor in need of a garden hose to put out a fire. After the fire was extinguished, he explained, the borrower would be expected to return the hose.

Over the next several weeks, Roosevelt took his case to Congress and the public in two notable speeches. The first came at the end of December in the form of a fireside chat. He assured listeners that he had no intentions of intervening in the war but viewed it as the responsibility of the United States to play a role in defeating Hitler through the production of goods and weaponry. The nation, he declared, was a peaceful one, but this did not mean it could sidestep its responsibilities to combat authoritarianism and dictatorship. The nation had to accept its duty as "the great arsenal of democracy." A few weeks later, Roosevelt addressed Congress in his annual state of the union address, where he delivered one of the more significant speeches of his presidency. Not only did he call for support of a lend-lease policy toward Great Britain; he also sought to outline the primary aims of U.S. foreign policy. Describing the Nazi regime as a threat to civilization, he proposed that the United States had a responsibility to promote "four freedoms" worldwide: freedom of speech, freedom of religion, freedom from want, and freedom from fear. The message hearkened back to Woodrow Wilson's appeal for international values that were to be assured through the League of Nations—his so-called Fourteen Points, many of which articulated the four freedoms Roosevelt described. Roosevelt's idealism resonated well with the public and played a significant role in winning over Congress to the policy of lend-lease. A bill passed both houses in early March that enhanced greatly U.S. military assistance to Great Britain.

Depressing news continued to filter in from Europe. England was teetering on the brink as a result of a furious air campaign the German *Luftwaffe* began months earlier; only an extraordinary amount of resolve on behalf of the British people prevented a complete collapse. Hitler followed up this assault with a prolonged and devastating submarine campaign intended to cut off England from the United States. Despite the increase of aid assured through lend-lease, the administration still operated under limitations imposed by the Neutrality Acts, which required the transportation of U.S. materials to Europe with British vessels. Roosevelt believed that the time had come for either a revision or, better yet, the abolition of the laws. The German navy could carry out its attacks at full throttle without risk of bringing the United States into the conflict. According to several accounts, the German führer already believed that United States' entry into the war was inevitable; however, there was little need to poke the American bear unnecessarily.

Interestingly, as these dispatches arrived in the United States, Roosevelt began to receive criticism from those who called for more action in protecting merchant vessels under attack by German U-boats. The loudest voices came from within the administration, as Secretary of War Henry L. Stimson, perhaps the most interventionist-minded figure in the cabinet, complained that the president's unwillingness to deploy U.S. gunboats to protect British ships was caused by fears of a political backlash from the isolationists. Now Stimson and a few others were calling on Roosevelt to declare war on Germany. This no-win situation left him at an impasse. For months, even years, Roosevelt had worked to enhance U.S. military presence in the Atlantic and drew repeated fire from isolationists in Congress. Now, more bellicose voices accused him of timidity rooted in political calculation.

This political logjam began to break up in the summer of 1941. In June, the trajectory of the entire war took a drastic turn when Hitler's forces plunged eastward into the Soviet Union. The abandonment of the Nazi-Soviet Pact did not come as a complete shock to Stalin; in fact, since the agreement of a year earlier, the Russian autocrat had been bolstering his defenses in anticipation of such an event. What did come as a complete surprise was the timing of the offensive, for Stalin believed that war with Germany only would commence if, and when, the Nazis defeated the British and their allies. As over three million German troops pounded their way through the Baltic States with ease, the government in Moscow reeled. In hindsight, Hitler's decision to invite a two-front war seemed a deadly mistake. At the time, there were strong reasons to believe that the Germans might actually prevail on both fronts.

Interventionists in Roosevelt's cabinet viewed the invasion of Soviet Russia as more evidence that circumstances demanded the United States enter the war. Stimson advised that a declaration of war against Hitler would be welcomed by the American public. Yet the president again demurred and even suggested that the Soviet Union's entry into the conflict might keep the United States out of the war altogether. The episode did alter the administration's policies, however, as Roosevelt now considered extending military assistance to the Russians. In the weeks that followed, Harry Hopkins traveled to Moscow to confer with Stalin, who revealed a strong need for U.S. hardware. By the end of the summer, the U.S. naval presence in the Atlantic had become more pronounced, as Roosevelt had every intention of supplying Stalin with as much weaponry as possible without compromising defenses at home. Through an agreement made with Denmark, Iceland now fell under the United States defense perimeter, which meant that U.S. gunboats would escort merchant vessels to within a few hundred miles of England. Roosevelt had managed to escalate the naval presence in the North Atlantic without directly violating the Neutrality Acts.

The move to extend U.S. defenses also may have been prompted by an August meeting between Roosevelt and Churchill at a hastily arranged conference off the Newfoundland coast. The prime minister was delighted to discover Roosevelt's strong commitment to seeing the Axis powers of Germany, Italy, and Japan defeated. Although the two men could not reach agreement on the United States' entry into the conflict, they did manage to draw up a document articulating Allied war aims. The so-called Atlantic Charter promoted the same principles that Roosevelt had introduced as the Four Freedoms in his January speech and was the strongest message of support for the war effort to date from the United

States government. Several observers back home considered it an unofficial declaration of war.

Hitler's navy may have read it as such. As the United States extended its defenses closer to Europe, U.S. ships became targets for the first time. On September 4, Roosevelt received word that a destroyer, the U.S.S. *Greer*, had received fire from a German submarine. Although the ship was not hit, the administration viewed the incident as a reason to call for an even larger deployment in the North Atlantic. On September 11, while mourning the death of his 86-year-old mother Sara, Roosevelt delivered a stinging address, describing Hitler's forces as a "rattlesnake poised to strike," and announced that all armed vessels would be given blanket orders to fire at will. In the following weeks, two more ships came under attack, the U.S.S. *Kearny* and the *Reuben James*. There were casualties in both incidents; the *Reuben James*, sunk off the coast of Iceland, lost its entire crew. The United States now was in a state of undeclared war with Germany.

Still mindful of public attitudes, however, Roosevelt decided against pressing for a formal war declaration. Even in the aftermath of the sinking of the *Reuben James*, polls indicated that a large majority of Americans opposed taking up arms against Hitler. Attitudes clearly were shifting, though, particularly in Congress, where denunciations of German aggression became commonplace. Perhaps Roosevelt also believed that war was inevitable. If so, there was little reason to hasten it. For the time being, he felt comfortable with the fact that U.S. ships were now free to defend themselves against attack. As long as the Allies were holding their own against the enemy, the country could continue to prepare before taking the plunge into a large-scale commitment.

Another reason for Roosevelt's cautious behavior had to do with circumstances in Asia. Already-strained relations had deepened when, in 1937, the Japanese launched a full-scale invasion of China. In September 1940, the government in Tokyo announced its alliance with Germany and Italy and its intentions of "liberating" all of the Pacific Rim from France and Great Britain. With France now under occupation, the Japanese had a perfect opportunity to capture Indochina without strong resistance. For the United States these developments meant that the two theatres were now linked inextricably. The German-Japanese alliance also caused the Allies considerable grief. If Great Britain were to divert forces away from Europe to protect its Pacific colonies, Hitler would gain an even greater advantage. The Soviets also were caught in this vice; the prospect of a

Japanese invasion of its Eastern regions was now conceivable, as Stalin needed every man available to fight Hitler on the European front.

Japan's aggression placed the administration in a precarious position as the "arsenal of democracy" in Europe. If war were to become a reality in the Pacific, U.S. military support for its Allies might have to decrease. Roosevelt's response early on was to seek ways of hindering the Japanese without sparking a conflict. The Pacific Fleet, stationed off the California coast, was moved to the naval base at Pearl Harbor in Hawaii. Defenses in the Philippines also were bolstered, and aid to China was increased. Strategically, the message the military hoped to send Japan was that war with the United States was a possibility—a message that would force Japan into a difficult two-front war with the United States and China.

With defenses improved, Roosevelt also turned to economic sanctions as a deterrent against the Japanese. The island nation, devoid of natural resources such as iron ore and petroleum, had long relied on trade with the United States and the colonial powers of Europe. During the 1930s, Japan bought more than three-fourths of its oil from the United States; an embargo of petroleum products was a powerful diplomatic sword that might be wielded. British and Dutch colonies in the East Indies, also oil-rich, joined the embargo, thus placing the Japanese military in a difficult, perhaps catastrophic, position. In response to these actions, Japanese Admiral Isoroku Yamamoto, commander of all naval forces, designed a bold strategy that called for an immediate strike against the United States designed to wipe out the Pacific Fleet. The embargo, in the minds of extremists, signified that war between the two nations was now inevitable.

More cautious voices in the Japanese government warned of the risks involved in attacking the United States; however, the newly installed premier, General Hideki Tojo, was a military hardliner who supported the plan. A fierce blow struck against the Pacific Fleet would leave the U.S. military in disarray; in the meantime, Japan could move quickly to secure possession of Indonesia and the Philippines. With this enhanced perimeter, and with Hitler making gains in Europe, the expectation was that the United States would seek a negotiated settlement, at least in the short run. Months of planning went into the assault, while the Japanese government continued to negotiate for an end to the sanctions.

Sunday, December 7, was a day marked by confusion, disbelief, and horror. News of an attack at Pearl Harbor arrived at the White House around 2:00 in the afternoon. Adding to the surreal mood of the day was the fact that, even as Roosevelt listened to details of the raid, two Japanese negotiators sat waiting outside the office of Secretary of State Hull to offer a new set of peace demands. The Japanese had blundered in their timing, hoping to deliver to Hull a formal rejection of the administration's most recent proposals immediately prior to the invasion. Instead, a dazed and outraged Hull, having been informed of the attack, allowed the delegation in and vented his anger at the surprised visitors. Meanwhile, Roosevelt called together his war cabinet. He also called Churchill to inform him that the United States was now at war. "We are all in the same boat now," he explained.

As Roosevelt designed a public response, word of the damage continued to filter in. The attack, which included about two hundred Japanese planes, had not destroyed the Pacific Fleet altogether, but the results were disastrous nonetheless. Nineteen ships were sunk, over two hundred American aircraft demolished, and more than 2,000 U.S. soldiers lay dead. The work that lay ahead was immense. Not only would these losses need to be recovered, but the Pacific navy would have to be strengthened far beyond its original size to carry the battle to Japan. The attack also meant that war in Europe would most likely commence. Roosevelt remained calm throughout the afternoon as he discussed strategies for mobilization with military advisors.

He also dictated a brief speech to Grace Tully, his longtime secretary, that he planned to deliver before Congress the next day. The mood at the Capitol that Monday morning was an eerie mixture of mourning, outrage, and conviction as Roosevelt made his way to the dais at the front of the House chamber amidst thunderous applause. The words were brief, but moving. "Yesterday, December 7, 1941—a date which will live in infamy—the United States of America was suddenly and deliberately attacked by naval and air forces of the Empire of Japan." He concluded his remarks with a request that Congress approve a declaration of war, which occurred later in the day. There no longer would be a need for the political finesse that marked Roosevelt's foreign policy for the past two years. On this day, Americans seemed united.

Critics of Roosevelt, at the time and especially later, claimed that he somehow orchestrated the attack in order to gain universal support for U.S. entry into the war against Hitler. There were blunders, to be sure. In the weeks leading up to the raid, intelligence reports suggested that Japanese forces were preparing for some sort of action. Military officials explained to Roosevelt that an attack, if it did occur, would take place in the South Pacific in an attempt by Japan to seize British and French possessions. Naval commanders had been on alert but not for an invasion of the U.S. territory of Hawaii. Roosevelt may have been guilty of taking the

Japanese threat too lightly, perhaps a result of the intense focus placed on events in Europe. If anything, Roosevelt's error in 1941 was inaction.

The first order of business was to establish a clear military command. Secretary of War Stimson continued to serve as primary liaison between the military brass and the White House. Despite Roosevelt's lifelong interest in diplomacy, he never held illusions that he would formulate military strategy in case of war. He did, however, expect to stay in close contact with his officers and surrounded himself with an able advisory team. General George Marshall, who had served as army chief of staff since September 1939, along with Navy Admiral Ernest J. King and Henry "Hap" Arnold of the Army Air Corps, became joint chiefs of staff charged with designing and implementing a grand strategy. Over time, Marshall and King emerged as the most influential of the team. Finally, Harry Hopkins, who at the time the war began was living in the White House, became a crucial diplomatic advisor. Roosevelt considered Hopkins indispensable and often dispatched him to meetings with Allied leaders in his stead.

Another pressing matter was the challenge of reorienting the economy for war production. Although military production had increased over the past two years to meet Allied demands, shortages in all areas were a serious problem. Not only would there be a need for extraordinary amounts of hardware—planes, tanks, jeeps, weapons, and ammunition—but also other products, such as food, clothing, and even clerical materials. In his 1942 state of the union address, which he delivered in January, Roosevelt offered preliminary figures that staggered the imagination: 60,000 more planes, 25,000 more tanks, and hundreds of new merchant vessels.

The rate of military production, in Roosevelt's view, had not been promising, as orders for equipment had been beleaguered by delays, cancelled contracts, and inefficiency. In an effort to enhance productivity, the White House announced in late January the creation of a War Production Board to oversee mobilization, headed by former Sears, Roebuck executive Donald M. Nelson. The agency eventually was complemented by an Office of War Mobilization, led by James F. Byrnes, a senator from South Carolina whom Roosevelt had appointed to the Supreme Court a year earlier. Byrnes gradually emerged as the primary economic planner for the administration, in charge of designing production schedules and overseeing the regulation of wages and prices.

Not surprisingly, Roosevelt's New Deal experiences guided his mobilization strategy. He envisioned a cooperative venture between government and private industry to meet defense needs. As had been the case with his recovery programs at the height of the Depression, industrialists and business leaders responded positively, for the most part. The greatest beneficiaries of mobilization were the largest of corporations, which were best poised to meet large and demanding production orders. There was some sensitivity to smaller businesses; Congress created a Smaller War Plants Corporation designed to broaden the number of participants in war contracting. Efforts to democratize defense bidding, however, could at times cause delays. On the whole, large corporations filled almost two-thirds of all war contracts.

Wartime production also required smooth labor-management relations, something that Roosevelt had learned during his service in the Department of the Navy during World War I. While patriotism pressured unions to avoid strikes and work stoppages, the administration also implemented policies to encourage cooperation between workers' organizations, business owners, and the government. The National War Labor Board was established to arbitrate disputes arising in war-related industries. The board also provided unions with incentives to work within the framework of mobilization policy, particularly the adoption of a "maintenance of membership" program that required workers who joined a union when hired to remain a member for the duration of their employment. Union membership, in fact, almost doubled during the war. By 1945, one-third of all U.S. workers were unionized—an all-time high. A number of unions also agreed to a "no-strike pledge" during the war in an effort to keep production speeding along. There were exceptions, most notably the actions of the fiery John L. Lewis, head of the United Mine Workers, who led a walkout of coal miners in 1943 that generated considerable public resentment. For the most part, however, labor cooperated in the administration's wartime efforts.

Massive increases in production caused concerns about wage and price inflation due to such a rapid rise in demand. An Office of Price Administration created ceilings for prices on manufactured goods and food. Wages were regulated through the War Labor Board. Roosevelt also made public appeals in support of wage controls. In a 1942 fireside chat, he explained the need for such policies in terms of national sacrifice. "The price for civilization," he admonished, "must be paid in hard work and sorrow and blood."

Funding the war also presented challenges. Early in his presidency, Roosevelt had pledged to maintain a balanced federal budget but gradually had come to accept government deficits in order to promote economic growth. Yet the massive increases in military spending required by the war might drive deficits to historic highs without increases in revenue.

In October 1942, the Revenue Act created new taxes that would raise over seven billion dollars each year, primarily through increased income tax rates. Between 1939 and 1942, the number of Americans who paid income taxes increased by a factor of ten, to over 40 million. The war also introduced the concept of automatic withholding of taxes from workers' paychecks to improve efficiency in collection. The United States Treasury also launched a massive advertising campaign to raise funds through the sale of war bonds. Henry Morgenthau, secretary of the treasury, promised Roosevelt in 1942 that he could raise an astonishing one million dollars per month through the sale of bonds and savings stamps—a goal that was achieved very early in the war.

Overall, the war proved to be a boon for the national economy. As the military mobilized the largest fighting force in U.S. history—some 12 million men and women served in the army alone—the demand for more workers erased the high unemployment figures that had dogged policy-makers for a decade. Cities teemed with new arrivals looking to fill job openings; larger numbers of women found their way into the workforce. African Americans, who had experienced much higher unemployment than the broader population, saw more work opportunities with better wages. The wartime economy also changed the demographic makeup of the country. Areas where defense-related industries flourished, such as the South and especially the West Coast, experienced rapid population increases and began growth trends that would continue for decades.

As the administration mobilized, both in economic and human terms, there also occurred the controversial decision to move Japanese Americans into internment camps due to fears of espionage and sabotage. In the weeks following the attack on Pearl Harbor, fears erupted that the presence of people of Japanese ancestry, particularly in concentrated neighborhoods in cities on the West Coast, were a threat to domestic security. Newspaper editorials fueled rumors that the Japanese government had planted agents in these areas that would rise up and attack Americans in coordination with raids carried out by the Japanese military. When the War Department requested authorization to remove these individuals, many of whom were U.S.-born citizens, out of designated military zones, Roosevelt approved the policy by issuing Executive Order 9066. Eventually, more than 100,000 people were forced to relocate to these camps. Roosevelt expressed some concern with the idea and at one point mentioned to Stimson, who criticized the move on grounds of civil liberties, that the program should be carried out with restraint. However, as was his policy in most military matters, the president deferred to his military advisors.

For those affected, internment was very difficult, as many were required to sell their homes and move into spartan, and sometimes quite harsh, relocation facilities. In later years the policy received criticism; however, at the time, public response was restrained. Few reporters paid attention to the story, and even the most ardent civil libertarians made little of these actions. The American Civil Liberties Union, which was formed during World War I due in part to perceived maltreatment of "enemy aliens," offered very little in the way of opposition. If Roosevelt had serious misgivings about the internment policy, he left little to indicate such concerns in his correspondence.

As mobilization continued apace, Roosevelt worked with the military command and the Allies to formulate a strategy for winning the war. Pearl Harbor notwithstanding, there was widespread agreement that the first priority was to slow down Hitler's advances in Europe. There was significant disagreement as to how this "Europe First" policy should proceed. Churchill, now consulting with Roosevelt on a regular basis, proposed an invasion of North Africa, which the Germans had seized in the early stages of the war. By forcing the Nazi military back across the Mediterranean, he believed, the enemy would lose important strategic positions and prevent any moves on crucial locations in the Middle East. Convinced that Churchill was correct, Roosevelt turned to the joint chiefs to discuss logistical planning for an invasion of Africa.

To his surprise, he discovered that his military commanders disagreed with Churchill and instead favored a full-scale invasion of Western Europe that would take the fight directly to Hitler. General Marshall, for whom Roosevelt had immense respect, believed Churchill's strategy to be flawed, arguing that an African campaign would drain resources and men to the periphery of the war. Marshall believed that Hitler's decision to invade the Soviet Union had been a crucial mistake that could be exploited if the Germans were forced to fight on two fronts. A coordinated British, French, and U.S. attack on the coast of France, he believed, would prove disastrous for the enemy.

Roosevelt also knew that the Soviets shared this desire for the opening of a Western front as soon as possible. Stalin had broached the subject early on in the war, when Hopkins had traveled to Moscow following Hitler's invasion of the country. In late May, Roosevelt met with Soviet Foreign Minister Vyacheslav Molotov, who related horrific stories of conditions in the country as Russian troops fought to hold the line against a far better equipped German military. In his gut, Roosevelt believed the Russians were right; he promised Molotov that an invasion across the English Channel would take place as soon as possible. Churchill, however, was insistent that the Allies were not ready to launch such an operation and continued to press for a move into Africa. Roosevelt vacillated, and the Russians interpreted his inaction as insincerity. The delay of a cross-channel invasion for at least a year generated mistrust on the part of Stalin toward his Western allies.

The White House remained deadlocked on how to proceed. Marshall, growing impatient, decided to force the issue by suggesting that the entire Europe First strategy be jettisoned and that a large-scale offensive in the Pacific be planned. He, along with King and Stimson, had hoped that this gambit would move Roosevelt off the fence and support an invasion of France. Instead, these actions had the opposite effect. Fearful of the eroding cooperation between Great Britain and the United States, Roosevelt sent his advisors to London to further discuss an African campaign. By the end of the trip, plans were being finalized for the offensive; General Dwight D. Eisenhower, head of the United States' European forces, described the beginning of the campaign as the "blackest day in history."

The standoff between Roosevelt and the military command over the North African campaign was not typical of relations between them, and any ill feelings generated during these months were short-lived. On the whole, he enjoyed a positive rapport with the joint chiefs, perhaps due to the fact that Roosevelt did his best to avoid micromanaging the war. From time to time, this hands-off approach sparked complaints of indecision, yet most commanders preferred Roosevelt's style of leadership that left generalship in the hands of generals. In the end, the joint chiefs accepted the North African plan and resolved to make the best of what they viewed as a somewhat flawed strategy.

Having made the decision to move into Africa, Roosevelt hoped to see the operation begin immediately. However, coordination and planning would take months. Throughout the summer of 1942, while waiting for the offensive to begin, he turned his attention to the Pacific, where Japanese advances had been stalled. Code breakers in the navy performed brilliantly in discovering Japanese plans to invade Midway Island on the heels of a heated confrontation at the Battle of the Coral Sea. Although U.S. forces were outnumbered, they were prepared for the attack and not only held the island, but also destroyed four enemy carriers. The setback sent a wave of caution through Admiral Yamomoto's command, while improving the outlook of the United States Navy, which was operating under the leadership of Admiral Chester W. Nimitz. In early August, U.S. forces took the island of Guadalcanal. Even with a Europe First strategy, the navy seemed to be making headway, thus buying even more time for defeating Hitler.

Finally, on November 8, 1942, General Eisenhower led some two hundred thousand troops onto the shores of Morocco and Algeria. At Casablanca, in Morocco, U.S. forces were confronted by French troops of the Vichy government, the German-allied state formed in Paris following the fall of that country. The sight of French troops aiding Hitler angered many Americans; however, neither Roosevelt nor Eisenhower wanted to fight the French unless absolutely necessary. In a decision that generated some controversy, Eisenhower struck a deal with the French commander, Admiral Jean Darlan, that recognized French rule in Morocco in exchange for an armistice. Although much of the American public grumbled about negotiating with Nazi allies, Roosevelt explained the move as an expedient. The American fight was with the Germans and Italians, not the French.

With North Africa on the way to being secured, Roosevelt and Churchill met to discuss a future strategy in Casablanca. Both men had hoped that Stalin would attend, but the Russian premier was unwilling to leave the dire situation within his country. In one of the more horrific, but also pivotal, battles of the war, German troops had laid siege to the city of Stalingrad. The city became a symbol of Russian resistance to the Nazi onslaught as its citizens braced for a prolonged ordeal. In January 1943, Roosevelt boarded a plane for Miami—the first president to fly in an aircraft. From there, the team, which included Harry Hopkins and Admiral Ross McIntire, flew to the Caribbean, then to Brazil, and ultimately ended the 7,000-mile journey in North Africa. The trip also marked the first time a president traveled outside the country during a time of war. According to Hopkins, Roosevelt displayed his typical boy-like enthusiasm during the entire trip.

There was much to discuss at the 10-day conference, particularly with respect to planning the next major military offensive. Marshall remained consistent in advocating a cross-channel invasion, but once again Churchill proposed another flanking maneuver—this time into Italy. The prime minister argued that an invasion of this "soft under-belly of Europe" would prove more successful than an invasion of France and would further weaken German defenses. Churchill also continued to believe that the Allies were not yet prepared to open a Western front. An attack from the south might force Hitler to divide his forces yet again, laying even more groundwork for a successful invasion in the west. Once again, the Western front would be delayed, this time until summer 1944.

With military plans finalized, Roosevelt finished off the conference with a proposal that surprised Churchill and generated controversy at home: a declaration that the Allies would accept nothing less than unconditional surrender from the Axis powers. His reasoning may have been to prevent the Germans from claiming that the country had not been defeated but rather "stabbed in the back" by internationalists, a myth that circulated in that country following World War I. The announcement also may have been a message intended for Stalin that the Allies would not seek a negotiated peace with Hitler or with Japan while the Soviet Union continued to fight. Roosevelt later claimed that the statement was not planned and that it simply came to him at the conference in a mood of resolve. Regardless of the motivations behind it, critics asserted that the policy of unconditional surrender may have lengthened the war by diminishing the possibility of negotiated settlement.

The next several months were a time of Allied gains in both the Atlantic and the Pacific. The Russians turned the tide by pushing back the Germans at Stalingrad following a 10-week siege that left hundreds of thousands dead. In the spring, Allied bombing raids on German cities took their toll on the ability of the Nazis to produce weaponry and on the resolve of the people. The combined naval forces of the United States and Great Britain also made great headway in controlling the high seas by destroying much of the German submarine deployment in the Atlantic. In the Pacific, the U.S. Navy was now on the offensive, adopting a policy of "island hopping" to push the Japanese back toward Tokyo.

In July 1943, Allied forces numbering almost five hundred thousand landed on the island of Sicily to launch the Italian campaign. They met much lighter resistance than expected and moved the timetable forward for an assault on the peninsula. On July 25, the people of Italy rose up and toppled Dictator Benito Mussolini, placing the government and military on shaky ground. Even as German forces entered northern Italy to shore up defenses, the new Italian leader, Marshal Pietro Badoglio, was negotiating surrender to the Allies. While fierce fighting with German troops would continue in northern Italy in the coming months, the campaign was a resounding success.

The frenzied schedule brought on by the war made life in the White House a far cry from the familial, and often jovial, atmosphere of Roosevelt's first two terms. Eleanor, who in typical fashion had plunged into her role as wartime first lady with a strong sense of commitment, seldom was in Washington. She continued her work in the area of civil rights, touring the country and speaking at an array of events. In the summer of 1942, she departed on a tour of the South Pacific with the Red Cross to visit the wounded. All four of the Roosevelt sons were serving overseas. On those rare occasions when Franklin had time to spend in the White House, he struggled to obtain much needed rest. He turned 60 years old in 1942, and, while he had no serious health problems, often he suffered from exhaustion or lingering illnesses, no doubt brought on by stress. Eleanor's diaries and letters from the period noted her husband's poor physical condition and the lack of cheerfulness that always had been a central part of his personality.

The war, however, drove him forward. In November 1943, with the tide clearly turning in favor of the Allies, Roosevelt, Churchill, and Stalin came together for the first meeting of the so-called Big Three. The site was Teheran, in Iran, as Stalin refused to travel far from home while German troops continued to threaten his country. On the way to Iran, Roosevelt stopped off at Cairo, Egypt, to confer with Chinese Nationalist leader Chiang Kai-shek, who was struggling to combat not only the Japanese forces in his country but also the growing army of Chinese Communist leader Mao Zedong. For years, Roosevelt had pinned strong hopes on Chiang's government, often suggesting that a strong and stable China was crucial for peace in Asia. Only months earlier, Chiang's aristocratic wife had visited the White House in an effort to strengthen ties between the two governments. The situation for Chiang was not good. The level of opposition to his government had grown dramatically over the past two years, as more and more peasants joined Mao's cause. Roosevelt discussed prospects for future cooperation between the two governments, which would be crucial for the Nationalists in winning the civil war that likely would erupt following the war with Japan. For now, however, Roosevelt's primary aim was to keep China in the war.

The conference in Teheran, which began in late November, packed into four hectic days a great deal of discussion regarding the future of the entire globe. Roosevelt had been excited about meeting the Soviet premier for the first time and described him to be quite approachable. The most immediate issue was to hammer out details for a cross-channel invasion. Stalin received an assurance that an offensive would begin the following spring. With respect to the Asian theatre, Stalin agreed to enter the war against Japan following the defeat of Hitler.

There also were larger issues pertaining to the postwar world order. Roosevelt explained to Stalin his views on a new international organization that would replace the now-defunct League of Nations. Preliminary discussions over the fate of Germany also occurred. While most of the proceedings went smoothly, there were some points of disagreement. Stalin, for example, made clear his intentions to play a strong role in organizing the government in Poland after the war and also to maintain control of the Polish territory acquired by the Soviets from the Nazi-Soviet Pact.

Churchill insisted that the Polish government-in-exile, which during the war operated from London, be allowed to return, a prospect Stalin received coolly. In all, however, the meeting was held in an atmosphere of cooperation. Roosevelt returned to Washington optimistic that a peaceful world order could be achieved in the aftermath of hostilities. In a fireside chat delivered after the conference, he described his vision of a world in which the major powers of the globe—Great Britain, the Soviet Union, China, and the United States—would work in harmony to guarantee peace and stability.

The success of the Teheran meeting also provided Roosevelt with confidence that the administration could now begin to plan America's own postwar future. His 1944 state of the union address offered an ambitious set of domestic goals to be pursued following the defeat of the Axis. One major theme of the speech was national unity. He suggested that the mobilization of the United States' people and resources achieved in wartime could be maintained during peacetime. He proposed a national service law, which would require all adult citizens to be made eligible for a draft for industrial labor or military service. He also discussed the possibilities of a new economic "bill of rights," which would guarantee economic security for all citizens. The first Bill of Rights, he explained, had offered protections of political liberty. Now, the list of enumerated rights should be expanded to include the right to food, clothing, and shelter; the right to medical care; the right to education; and the right to be protected from indigence brought on by old age, sickness, or unemployment.

These ideas for reform were unprecedented in their breadth and served as an indication that Roosevelt had every intention to strengthen and expand the New Deal despite the fact that the Depression had come to an end. His goals also were intentionally vague, for Roosevelt was seeking to reorient attitudes about government rather than offer a specific list of reform initiatives to be debated in Congress. The strong rhetoric also implied that he intended to run for a fourth term later in the year. In contrast to 1940, there was little mystery regarding his plans. As long as the war continued, he believed that the nation needed consistency in the White House. Roosevelt was drained, physically and perhaps emotionally, and the prospects of finishing the war and yet another campaign season must have given him pause. However, he was convinced that the United States needed his leadership and experience at such a pivotal time.

Chapter 11

HOME AGAIN

By the time Roosevelt returned from Teheran, Americans were anticipating an end to war, as rumors spread that it might be over by spring. Although the Allies were making real progress, these hopes were unrealistic. The United States had made notable headway in the Pacific, but, as troops pushed closer to Japan, resistance became increasingly stiff. In Europe, there was still the massive undertaking of a cross-channel invasion. Clearly, however, the past year had brought positive gains. The battered Russians were now turning back German forces. The Italians were now out of the war. Japan was on its heels. Even as the U.S. military began serious planning for an invasion of the French coast, which was now scheduled for summer 1944, war production was scaled back and discussions regarding retooling the economy back to peacetime status began.

With the war going well, Roosevelt turned his attention to domestic issues that might be distractions during the upcoming election campaign. Although the administration's labor policies had been successful in encouraging productivity and cooperation, cracks were beginning to appear. In December 1943, railroad workers announced their intentions to strike for wage increases. Negotiations made little headway. The National War Labor Board feared that a substantial raise for these workers could trigger even more disruption as other unions would seek improvements as well. After Christmas, Roosevelt, growing impatient with the lack of progress in talks between labor leaders and government officials, announced that he was prepared to take over operations of the rails as a wartime necessity. The action sparked more complaints among militant unionists and accusations that the administration was interfering with the rights of workers to bargain. Yet the strong stance did the trick, as the threat of nationalization forced the hands of militants, who began to negotiate. By the end of January, the dispute was over.

Another problem was the increasingly conservative orientation of Congress. The Republicans had made gains in the 1942 elections, and Roosevelt could no longer count on support of his domestic programs. His lofty 1944 state of the union address was intended not only to reaffirm the New Deal but to expand it into new areas. Walter Lippmann, who had spent much of the past decade taking jabs at the administration, now praised Roosevelt for his willingness to take on unpopular issues, which seemed to him a departure from his tendency to take positions based on political calculation rather than conviction. The reception of the speech among legislators was much more cool, however, and in the weeks following the speech several congressional leaders made it clear that they had no plans to rubber-stamp Roosevelt's reform programs. The climate was a far cry from the Hundred Days of a decade earlier, when Congress had been easily managed. Now, the rift between the two branches of government was such that Roosevelt would have to fight for every vote and also show willingness to compromise.

One example of the shift in the political atmosphere was the heated debate over taxation that occurred in early 1944. The first salvo in the battle took place when Roosevelt sent a bill to Congress designed to increase the social security tax, which was promptly and soundly defeated in the Senate. In an attempt to counter the vast increases in government spending caused by the war, Roosevelt then proposed a new revenue bill that included significant increases in income tax rates. The House issued its own version with much lower rates—so low that Roosevelt vetoed the bill that arrived on his desk. He delivered a strongly worded veto message to Congress to scold what he considered to be lawmakers' irresponsible behavior. The new budget, he claimed, was guilty of benefiting "not the needy but the greedy." Although he had been able to use the bully pulpit in such showdowns in the past, in this case the strategy went awry, as Congress overrode the veto—the first time in history that a president's revenue bill had been overturned. The battle of taxation was perhaps the strongest indication that Roosevelt would experience a rocky road when dealing with the legislature.

To Roosevelt's dismay, the defeat over the revenue bill was followed by even greater challenges on the labor front. For years, his strategy of seeking middle ground between militant labor leaders who opposed heavy regulation and conservatives who called for even stronger measures had been effective. As opinion became more polarized, this course was more difficult to pursue. Concerned with the potential for strike activity to undermine the war, Congress a year earlier had passed a bill, over Roosevelt's veto, that empowered the government to take over the operation of industries considered crucial for the war if strikes threatened a slowdown. The measure placed upon the administration the task of making difficult decisions of when, and if, to use this newly acquired power, which could alienate the politically powerful labor movement. In 1944, Roosevelt considered a takeover of Montgomery Ward, which was spiraling toward a standoff between unionists and its strongly anti-union president, Sewell Avery. In response, Avery fumed to the press, describing Roosevelt as a dictator in the mold of Hitler.

In the midst of this volatile political climate, Roosevelt found the prospects of launching an ambitious social reform agenda discouraging at best. He was forced to mark time on his plans to create an economic bill of rights, which had been the centerpiece of his state of the union speech. Now, somewhat in retreat, the administration supported a program to aid war veterans, which he dubbed the GI Bill of Rights. He assumed, quite correctly as it turned out, that, while public support for government involvement in the areas of education, health care, and other areas of social welfare for the general public might be lacking, programs designed to aid soldiers returning from the battlefield would be strong. The Servicemen's Readjustment Act, signed into law in June, provided federal subsidies for education, health care, and home financing for veterans. In the years following World War II, millions took advantage of these programs.

These political challenges, combined with the stress of the war, took their toll on Roosevelt's health. Episodes of fatigue that had plagued him for years now became more frequent, and illnesses were easily contracted and difficult to overcome. Family members noticed that he often was out of breath, even following limited physical activity, and he experienced bouts of shaking. At the urging of his daughter Anna, his physician, Admiral Ross McIntire, agreed to send him to the naval hospital at Bethesda, Maryland, for a complete checkup. The results were not encouraging. Doctors noted his alarmingly high blood pressure, heart disease, mild cardiac failure due to an enlarged heart, and bronchitis. He was placed on a strict diet and ordered to get much more rest each day. At the doctors' suggestion, he also decided to take an extended vacation at Hobcaw, South Carolina, where he remained for a month.

Like those around him, Roosevelt was aware of his condition but elected to downplay it. Since his bout with polio two decades earlier, he

had developed a sensitivity regarding his health, believing that his fitness could become a political issue if publicized. His month-long respite
sparked rumors that he was near death; news that he had contracted can-
cer appeared in print. When he returned to Washington, the press was
waiting with questions about his ability to carry out his duties. In carefully
crafted appearances, the administration sought to placate any fears that
he would not be strong enough to serve another term in office. Admiral
McIntire also issued a series of public statements attesting to Roosevelt's
sound health.

These setbacks notwithstanding, Roosevelt continued to enjoy strong
public support, and the Republicans faced the unenviable task of selecting
a challenger in the upcoming election. This time, New York Governor
Thomas Dewey, who had achieved local fame in the 1930s as a young attorney by bringing high-profile gangsters to justice, emerged as the front-
runner. Only 42 years old, Dewey seemed Roosevelt's polar opposite in
style and mannerisms. He struck a somewhat elitist pose, usually dressed
in dapper fashion and seldom exhibiting the warmth and personality that
had become Roosevelt's strengths as a politician. Politically, Dewey was
in almost lockstep agreement with the president on the war and U.S. foreign policy generally. With little to distinguish the two candidates beyond
personality, the young challenger faced an uphill battle.

There was little reason to challenge the administration on the country's
involvement in the war. U.S. naval forces were making steady progress in
the Pacific, to the point that military commanders were now contemplating an invasion of Japan. In Europe, Stalin's armies had taken on the
brunt of the Nazi war machine and now were celebrating a string of desperately needed victories. On June 6, 1944, Allied forces finally launched
an assault onto the coast of France, at Normandy. D-Day was an extraordinary military undertaking that included 175,000 soldiers, 5,000 ships,
and 6,000 aircraft. Following intense resistance from entrenched German
defenses, the Allies managed to establish a beachhead and moved inland.
Hitler now faced the specter of a two-front war that would prove insur-
mountable.

Dewey also seemed to support the president on matters of international
relations. Roosevelt had pushed for the creation of a new congress of nations to replace the now-defunct League of Nations; years of discussion
and planning had yielded a preliminary model for a United Nations. In
August, an international conference took place in Washington, D.C.,
that hammered out many of the details regarding the organization. The
UN seemed to blend two different philosophies about how peace and sta-

bility could be ensured. In some respects it mirrored the design of the old League, for the blueprint called for the creation of an international assembly in which all nations would have representation. The major departure from the previous attempt at such a body was the concept of the Security Council, which gave the major powers of the world—the United States, Great Britain, the Soviet Union, and Nationalist China—veto power over the assembly. This change indicated a dose of realism that some countries were in a stronger position to guarantee peace and security than others. Roosevelt believed the UN was a vast improvement over the old League and spoke strongly in support of U.S. participation. Dewey agreed, and, while there was isolationist opposition to the joining the organization out of fear of relinquishing national sovereignty to an international organization, the Republican candidate did not make the UN an issue in the campaign.

The outcome of the election may never have been in serious doubt, as polls indicated strong leads for Roosevelt in all parts of the country. Yet there was some drama during the campaign. One source of interest was the matter of the president's running mate. Vice President Wallace, handpicked by Roosevelt during the 1940 campaign, had become an albatross around the administration's neck as he became a target of sharp criticism by conservative party members, particularly in the South. Roosevelt remained loyal to Wallace but gradually came to agree that there was no reason to create a civil war in the party over the matter. Several replacements were vetted. James Byrnes, who had been head of the Office of War Mobilization, seemed the clear front-runner. Yet he had his share of enemies in the party and within the administration. Roosevelt reckoned that if Wallace, whom he admired, had to be replaced, the new candidate had to be free of political baggage.

In the weeks prior to the Democratic convention, party leaders in consultation with Roosevelt turned to relative-unknown Harry S Truman, a Missouri senator. He was an attractive choice for several reasons. Truman's modest voting record would generate little opposition from southern conservatives, he had few political enemies, and as a border-state politician presumably he would not alienate elements of any wing of the party. He also seemed down-to-earth, in contrast to the idealistic Wallace. Truman had served in World War I, had worked in the men's clothing business, and was a far cry from the intellectualized figures that raised the ire of many in the party outside Washington. Nevertheless, Truman had been a strong supporter of the New Deal and was viewed favorably by labor unionists. Roosevelt did not know him well but agreed that the Missourian would be an asset to the ticket. At the convention, held in Chicago, Roosevelt and Truman received near-unanimous support.

The campaign for a fourth term was rocky from the outset. Following an extended tour in the Pacific, where Roosevelt consulted with naval commanders in Hawaii, he docked at Bremerton, Washington, in Puget Sound to deliver a campaign speech. Weak from his various illnesses, on-lookers were stunned by his gaunt features and disheveled appearance. His speech rambled with awkward pauses and stammers. In later years, one of his doctors disclosed that he actually had suffered a severe angina attack during the event, which caused sharp pains in his upper body. The incident raised even more questions about his fitness. News reports suggested that he might not be up to the task of leading the country through the war. While Dewey could hardly in good taste ask such questions, such speculation could prove helpful in his challenge for the presidency.

Another issue, which began as an isolated and seemingly trite incident, surprised Roosevelt as it grew into a nuisance. A rumor erupted that following a stop in the Aleutian Islands during his Pacific tour, Roosevelt's dog, Fala, had been left behind and that Roosevelt had dispatched a destroyer to retrieve the pet. Opponents pressed the matter, implying that the president had compromised defense security for a personal and trivial concern. Realizing the interest in the affair, newspaper reporters soon released another story, this one involving Roosevelt's daughter Anna, who allegedly had insisted on transporting her husband's dog on an airplane that resulted in removing wounded soldiers returning home from the flight. The campaign team found themselves confronting a barrage of questions about these events. In the end, however, Roosevelt had the last laugh when he gave a speech that included tongue-in-cheek remarks about the incident. He explained to an amused audience that, while his family did not mind such trivial attacks, "Fala does resent them." He continued the jest. "You know, Fala is Scotch … his Scotch soul was furious. He has not been the same since." The humor undercut the criticism surrounding the event and painted his opponents as unreasonable.

Surprisingly, the "Fala speech" revived the campaign, and any concerns about reelection were dispelled during the few weeks prior to election day due to a wave of good news. In late October, troops led by General Douglas MacArthur established a beachhead in the Philippines, followed soon by reports of a rout of Japanese forces at the Battle of Leyte Gulf. Roosevelt, enjoying a period of good health, mustered strength to close the campaign with a series of excellent speeches. The most memorable may have been in Chicago, where he stood before an audience of more than 100,000 and offered a fiery response to critics who seemed to support the administration's policies while attacking the president himself—a clear attack on Dewey. Other appearances, in New York and Boston, were important in answering questions of his flagging health. Considering the reality of his condition, which was quite poor, these performances were heroic.

For the fourth time in his career, Roosevelt ended a long presidential campaign by casting his vote in Hyde Park on election day. That evening, a parade of supporters bearing torch lights gathered at the family home and cheered uproariously when Roosevelt came out to greet them. He stayed up late receiving election returns. In the end, he received 53.3 percent of the popular vote to Dewey's 46 percent—a clear victory but also the closest election since 1916. The electoral vote count, however, was not nearly as close, as Roosevelt outdistanced his opponent 432-99, exceeding Roosevelt's own expectations. Jubilant, he returned to Washington to begin discussions of an endgame for the war. The campaign, however, had exhausted him. His blood pressure continued to remain at dangerously high levels, and he had lost more than 20 pounds in the prior few months. In late November, he retreated to Warm Springs to recover. He returned after three weeks of relaxation, resolved to press on despite a nagging lack of energy.

Inauguration Day 1945 was a solemn event keeping with the mood of war that pervaded Washington. The weather was dismal, as the day was greeted by snow and sleet. Roosevelt, still without the vigor to which Americans had grown accustomed, gave a very brief speech. He quoted words from his recently deceased schoolmaster from Groton, Rector Peabody, and called for international cooperation to guarantee peace. Later in the day, he met with his son James to discuss his will and reportedly considered arrangements for his funeral. He managed to get through an evening reception with high spirits, at least outwardly.

Just days following the inauguration, he embarked on another grueling journey, this time to a meeting of the Big Three in the distant Crimean port city of Yalta. The trip, which required several days at sea aboard a cruiser, the *Quincy*, ended with a rough flight from Malta in the Mediterranean Sea to the resort on the Black Sea. He was drained to the point that his British counterparts who met him at the airport in Yalta were startled by his appearance. There was much to discuss. Roosevelt wanted to receive assurances from Stalin that the Soviets would enter the war against Japan after the defeat of Germany. Despite the progress made by the U.S. Navy, Japanese troops still held key positions in Asia, including

Indonesia and mainland China. He was aware that an invasion of Japan would be difficult and likely to result in massive casualties. Russian entry into the conflict might hasten the war's end, perhaps by encouraging the Japanese government to surrender before such an assault would be necessary.

There was also the question of Soviet acceptance of the United Nations, which concerned Roosevelt a great deal. Stalin's Foreign Minister Molotov had attended the Washington, D.C., conference but proved to be a difficult negotiator. The Soviets had thrown a wrench into deliberations by insisting that all 16 of its republics be granted a vote in the general assembly; Roosevelt was now relieved to hear that Stalin was willing to compromise. The Soviet leader proposed that his nation have three votes, one for each of the major republics. Roosevelt knew that such a scenario would not be received well back home but nonetheless believed that the organization had to move forward and agreed to keep the question open. As Woodrow Wilson had learned decades earlier, compromise over ideals was necessary to garner support from all parties.

The most difficult negotiations focused on the future of Europe, particularly those regions now occupied by Soviet troops. The immediate problem was the fate of Poland, which perhaps took on greater significance at the conference because the settlement of this question might set a precedent for later negotiations over other areas of Eastern Europe. Roosevelt's expectations of Atlantic Charter principles of democracy and national self-determination for Poland faced a stringent challenge from Stalin, who seemed much more interested in the national security of the Soviet Union. The Soviets had no intention of giving up Polish territory gained as a result of the Nazi-Soviet Pact of 1940. Roosevelt, frustrated by the unyielding stance of Stalin and Molotov, gradually accepted that negotiation would be pointless.

The more crucial question, in Roosevelt's eyes, was the government in Poland after the war. Churchill agreed that an interim government should be established that contained elements of the Polish government-in-exile, stationed in London. Stalin already had assembled a pro-Communist state in the Polish city of Lublin and suggested that the country would become a close ally of the Soviet Union. In the end, Stalin agreed to general language that called for free elections to be held as soon as possible, but there were few guarantees in the document that the Soviets would relinquish control if the people voted for a Western-oriented government. Over the next few years, the Soviets made clear their intentions to dominate Poland. Elections were not held until 1947, and these were rigged to favor the Communists.

In retrospect, critics complained that Roosevelt had been a poor negotiator at Yalta regarding Poland. Agreements with Stalin over territory
in East Asia generated even more controversy. Stalin indicated before
the conference his desire to reclaim regions north of Japan, in particular
the Kurile Islands and part of Sakhalin. Roosevelt issued no objections
to these demands but hesitated when Stalin also proposed Soviet access
to warm-water ports in China. Russia held firm to its demands, pointing
out that it deserved something in exchange for willingness to enter the
war against Japan. Roosevelt finally relented by approving a general statement that the Soviets would have an "open door" to Chinese territory.
While he had given in on some matters, Roosevelt returned home in a
triumphant mood, believing that the agreement was a sign of future cooperation between the United States and the Soviet Union. In the State
Department, a number of officials complained that the Yalta agreements
had set dangerous precedents by encouraging Stalin to take a hard line
with the Americans.

On the return voyage, Roosevelt landed in Egypt, where he met briefly
with King Farouk of Egypt, Ethiopian Emperor Haile Selassie, and King
Ibn Saud of Saudi Arabia aboard a cruiser docked in the Suez Canal. Discussions over the fate of Jewish refugees in Europe became a point of conflict between Roosevelt and the Saudi king. Since the early stages of the
war, the Allies had come to learn the horrible details of Hitler's Final Solution, which resulted in the deaths of six million Jews. Like most Americans, Roosevelt had received rumors of the Holocaust with disbelief but
with time came to accept the bitter truth. The slow reaction to the Nazis'
extermination program proved costly for European Jewry. Roosevelt did
approve, in 1942, the creation of a War Refugee Board to help repatriate
those who escaped the death camps. As the war neared conclusion, Roosevelt supported the cause of Zionism, the plan of establishing a Jewish
state in the near-eastern region of Palestine.

In what Roosevelt probably considered a minor point at the time, he
broached the subject of Jewish settlements in Palestine with King Saud.
He was unprepared for Saud's response, who strongly opposed the entire
idea and instead suggested that Jewish refugees return to their country of
origin. The firm resolve of the Saudi king to keep Jews out of the Middle
East gave Roosevelt pause; he discussed with aids his plans to return to
Washington to fashion a new strategy to prevent the situation from esca-
lating into violence.

The journey to Yalta drained him. Those who were close to Roosevelt
often commented that his mood seemed to rise and fall with his physical
condition; by February he seldom felt well. Moreover, the atmosphere in

the White House was gloomy. There had been several losses in recent months. Missy LeHand, his personal secretary, on whom he had depended not only for professional assistance but also companionship, passed away while Roosevelt was touring the Pacific. Another close advisor and friend, Edwin "Pa" Watson, died just as Roosevelt was arriving home from Yalta. Harry Hopkins, now very ill, was hospitalized. Combined with the recent deaths of his mother and Rector Peabody, a sense of loss had become a constant in his life. Eleanor continued to be a friend, but the distance that had grown between them over the years was such that he could not count on her to fill these voids in his life.

The next few weeks were trying. He continued to monitor events of the war while battling poor health. He was troubled by news that Stalin seemed to be consolidating Communist control in Poland and now refused to allow Western observers into the country. With the cooperative mood of Yalta now a distant memory, the Soviet premier also downplayed the importance of the United Nations and suggested that Molotov might not attend an upcoming conference in San Francisco. Roosevelt complained privately that Stalin seemed intent on breaking every promise made just weeks before. In another ominous sign, Stalin also accused Great Britain and the United States of negotiating a secret peace with Germany while ignoring the eastern front. The claim was baseless and intended to fuel mistrust toward the Allies within his own country and perhaps to justify a larger military presence in East Germany.

These pressures became too great to bear, and in mid-March he agreed to take a trip to Warm Springs for a month of recuperation. Unable to eat, his weight dropped even more, and his blood pressure levels sapped him of strength to the point that making it through a day's tasks proved difficult. He arrived on March 30 and for a few days felt better. On most mornings, he attended to official business, reading reports from Washington and dictating letters to Grace Tully. He announced to the press his plans to return to the White House in time to attend the San Francisco conference of the United Nations, which was scheduled for April 25.

During these weeks, guests came and went. His cousin, Polly Delano, and her close friend and distant relative, Daisy Suckley, who had become regulars in the White House during the war years, arrived to provide him companionship. Also there was Lucy Mercer Rutherford, whose husband had died a few years earlier and had again become a friend to the president. Also there was Elizabeth Shoumatoff, who had arrived with Rutherford in order to paint Roosevelt's portrait. As he had preferred throughout his life, Roosevelt was surrounded by doting women. Eleanor remained in Washington.

The morning of April 12 began as any other. Roosevelt had slept late, because he had dined late the prior evening with Henry Morgenthau. His doctor arrived in the morning for a daily checkup; he reported feeling well other than suffering a nagging headache. In the early afternoon, he sat by the cabin's fireplace signing letters while Shoumatoff worked on his portrait. Just after one o'clock, he commented to Miss Suckley in a low voice that he "had a terrific headache," then slumped forward and fell unconscious. The women, in a panicked state, called for his doctor, who explained that the president had suffered a massive brain hemorrhage. For a couple of hours, he lay unconscious in bed, breathing heavily. Then, at 3:35, the breathing stopped. Franklin Roosevelt was dead at the age of 63.

Eleanor received word from Warm Springs by telephone that her husband had fallen unconscious and planned to board a plane for Georgia in the evening. A second call confirmed that he had died, and she spent the remainder of the day calling family and close friends. She also met briefly with Harry Truman, who had arrived promptly at the White House and asked if there was anything he could do for the family. Her memorable response was to ask the new president if she could do anything for him. Truman took the oath of office as Eleanor and much of the White House staff and cabinet looked on.

Despite public awareness of Roosevelt's declining health, the news of his death came as a shock to millions. Bells tolled across the country; flags flew at half-mast. Schools closed as Americans began a period of mourning. For many, Roosevelt's name had become synonymous with the presidency; it was difficult to imagine anyone else in the office. Churchill received the news with sadness and he explained to an American broadcaster in London that "one day the world, and history, will know what it owes your president." Stalin also was moved in his own way, responding to the news with a wire to the State Department urging an investigation into the death for fear that Roosevelt might have been poisoned.

From Warm Springs, Roosevelt's body was transported by train to Washington. Eleanor rode along, looking out at the crowds of mourners who lined tracks all along the way. A funeral service took place in the White House following a parade down Pennsylvania Avenue attended by thousands. Then Roosevelt's casket traveled to Hyde Park, where he was buried at the home of his youth.

Chapter 12

AFTERWORD

Franklin Roosevelt's place in history was a topic of discussion long before his death. The issue, in fact, was one for which he showed considerable sensitivity. He instructed his staff to preserve all documents and correspondences from his presidency and made arrangements himself for the construction of a presidential library, which became the first of its kind. To those who were not fond of Roosevelt, such behavior was an indication of his inflated sense of self or, worse, an attempt to revise public understanding of his leadership. Such criticism has an element of truth, for Roosevelt did take considerable time to edit many of these documents before they entered the public record. On the other hand, Roosevelt's actions also indicated an example of his belief in public service. The American people of the future, he sincerely believed, had a right to see for themselves the proceedings of his administration.

The controversy over Roosevelt's motives regarding his presidential records were but one of several controversies that followed him beyond the grave. Historians have come to agree almost universally that the New Deal did not achieve its goal of economic recovery. His supporters often take the view that his greatest contribution as president was an ability to provide confidence to the American public at a time of crisis. Critics and supporters alike have pointed to the New Deal as the beginnings of the modern welfare state. There were significant long-term reforms passed during his four terms in office, the Social Security Act perhaps the most far-reaching. Yet both camps at times have been guilty of overestimating Roosevelt's hand in designing the reforms of the New Deal. Much of the recovery program passed during the Hundred Days and after was based on concepts that had been discussed for years, if not decades. Furthermore, he often played a reactive role as president, approving programs and policies designed in the Congress or by his brain trust.

However, if Roosevelt was not the sole architect of the New Deal, his presidency did mark an increase in the power of the executive branch. There had been predecessors who at times broadened the scope of presidential authority, such as Andrew Jackson, Abraham Lincoln, and Theodore Roosevelt. The Roosevelt years were pivotal in establishing the modern presidency as the strongest of the three branches of national government. The New Deal placed responsibility for ensuring economic prosperity in the hands of the president, a trend that continued into the future. In the realm of foreign policy, the White House became the focal point of policy, at the expense of congressional authority. These new powers brought with them heightened responsibility—a fact that Roosevelt's successors would learn very well.

Other historians have pointed out the degree to which Roosevelt transformed the political aspects of the presidency. Always sensitive to his public image, he viewed the press as an important extension of the office and worked to cultivate a positive relationship with reporters. More than any president before him, his public persona often was controlled and scripted; future presidents followed suit. Although he was not a particularly gifted public speaker, he did have excellent speech writers and learned to use the medium of radio to his advantage. In later years, the advent of television offered presidents even greater opportunities to shape their public image through mass media. However, few were as adept in this area as Roosevelt. His use of polling data to gauge public opinion also set trends for the office that became standard practice in later years.

Roosevelt's wartime leadership has generated less criticism and controversy, but even here disagreements persist regarding his leadership abilities. The image of Roosevelt guiding the ship of state through World War II almost single-handedly was challenged by historians in later years. In many cases, he was a reactive president when it came to foreign affairs. He deferred many important military decisions to his advisors, and, while he negotiated directly with the other members of the Big Three at the major wartime conferences, he relied a great deal on his staff to formulate policy. While some historians have criticized Roosevelt for indecision and vacillation in the months following the outbreak of the war, others have applauded his cautious approach and ability to strike a balance in the midst of an increasingly polarized American public. The Cold War that came after his death has generated much debate as to Roosevelt's role in bringing on the conflict. Here, the record is cloudy also. At times he may have overestimated his ability to win Stalin over to cooperation. However, the circumstances were quite different before the war than after. Historians can only speculate on how he would have dealt with the challenges of the postwar world, had he lived through his fourth term.

Much of the fascination with Roosevelt as a historical subject might be tied to his complicated personality. The warmth he displayed before the American people seldom appeared to those who knew him closely. He was an outgoing man who thrived on companionship but who seemed to have few close friends. Descriptions of Roosevelt from those who knew him well run the gamut and often were contradictory. He was gregarious, but often withdrawn. He was idealistic, but often acted with sober realism. He was fond of frivolity but was often described as overly calculating. Attempts to locate the "real" Roosevelt have filled thousands of pages of biographies.

In the end, Franklin Roosevelt was a man for his age. He arrived on the national stage with unbridled optimism at a time when the national mood was dark. For a country hungry for action, he delivered with a deluge of reform programs. When Europe fell into chaos, Americans saw Roosevelt as a strong-willed and mature leader. Loved by his supporters and reviled by his detractors, he was the most influential political figure of his age.

BIBLIOGRAPHIC ESSAY

Scholarship on Franklin Roosevelt's life and career is vast and can be overwhelming. There have been more books and articles written about him than any other president, and each year the number grows. Historians continue to be fascinated by his personality and leadership, while his handling of the Great Depression and World War II continues to generate debate. For the most part, interpretations of Roosevelt's presidency have been favorable, although recently more critical examinations have appeared.

Fortunately for students of the man and his times, there are several extensive collections of primary documents that may be consulted to get a firsthand look at his life. A four-volume collection of private correspondence was compiled by his son Elliott Roosevelt, *FDR: His Personal Letters* (New York: Duell, Sloan, and Pearce, 1947–50). Another vast source is Samuel Rosenman, ed., *The Public Papers and Addresses of Franklin D. Roosevelt*, 13 vols. (New York: Random House, 1938–50). Another useful source is *The Complete Presidential Press Conferences of Franklin D. Roosevelt*, 25 vols. (New York: Da Capo, 1972). Also useful are the large number of books written by those who knew Roosevelt personally. Eleanor Roosevelt's two memoirs have much to say about her husband: *This Is My Story* (New York: Harper & Row, 1937) and *This I Remember* (New York: Harper & Row, 1949). Other accounts include Rexford Tugwell's *The Democratic Roosevelt* (Baltimore: Penguin, 1969 [1957]), Frances Perkins's *The Roosevelt I Knew* (New York: Viking, 1946), William Hassett's *Off the Record with FDR, 1942–1945* (New Brunswick, NJ, 1958), and Harold Ickes's *The Secret Diary of Harold Ickes*, 3 vols. (New York: Simon

& Schuster, 1953–4). Most of these were written by Roosevelt loyalists, and, while at times, offer criticism, they are for the most part positive accounts. For a more negative take, see James A. Farley, *Jim Farley's Story: The Roosevelt Years* (New York: Whittlesey House, 1948).

There also are a large number of biographies that seek to tell the life story of Roosevelt. Frank Freidel, who spent much of his career researching and writing about FDR, offered perhaps the most impressive work in a four-volume series, *Franklin D. Roosevelt, The Apprenticeship, The Ordeal, The Triumph, and Launching the New Deal* (Boston: Little, Brown, 1952–1973). These works trace Roosevelt's life from birth to his election to the presidency in startling detail. Freidel also published *Franklin D. Roosevelt: A Rendezvous with Destiny* (Boston: Little, Brown, 1990), which covers his entire life in one volume but focuses much more on his days in the White House. Arthur M. Schlesinger, Jr.'s three-volume biography, *The Age of Roosevelt* (Boston: Houghton Mifflin, 1957–60) focuses more on politics than on Roosevelt's personal life. Both Freidel and Schlesinger Roosevelt's leadership and favor the reforms launched during the New Deal. A more balanced investigation of Roosevelt's presidency is James MacGregor Burns, *Roosevelt: The Lion and the Fox* (New York: Harcourt, Brace, Jovanovich, 1956). Patrick Maney, *The Roosevelt Presence: A Biography of Franklin D. Roosevelt* (New York: Twayne, 1992) is an excellent brief account that offers a balanced examination of his career. Nathan Miller, *FDR: An Intimate History* (New York: Doubleday, 1983) is a well-written account that offers a great deal of personal information about Roosevelt and the family. For a discussion of Roosevelt's legacies and their impact on future presidents, see William E. Leuchtenberg, *In the Shadow of FDR: From Harry Truman to Ronald Reagan* (Ithaca, NY: Cornell University Press, 1983).

Another useful way to learn about Roosevelt is to consult the many books that examine portions of his career. On his early life, in addition to volume one of Freidel, see Kenneth S. Davis, *FDR: The Beckoning of Destiny, 1882–1928* (New York: Putman, 1971) and Geoffrey C. Ward, *Before the Trumpet: Young Franklin Roosevelt, 1882–1905* (New York: Harper & Row, 1989). An interesting account of Roosevelt's bout with polio is Hugh Gregory Gallagher, *FDR's Splendid Deception* (New York: Dodd, Mead, 1985). For accounts of Roosevelt's experiences as governor of New York, Kenneth Davis's *FDR: The New York Years, 1928–1933* (New York: Random House, 1985) is useful, along with volume three of Freidel. For coverage of the New Deal, William E. Leuchtenberg, *Franklin D. Roosevelt and the New Deal, 1933–1940* (New York: Harper & Row, 1963) is the standard by which others are measured. Volumes two and three of Schlesinger's trilogy, *The Coming of the New Deal* and *The Politics of Upheaval*, are good sources. See also Alonzo L. Hamby, *For the Survival of Democracy: Franklin Roosevelt and the World Crisis of the 1930s* (New York: Free Press, 2004). A vast literature on the United States during the Depression offers much about Roosevelt's leadership. See Anthony J. Badger, *The New Deal: The Depression Years, 1933–1940* (New York: Farrar, Straus and Giroux, 1989), and Robert S. McElvaine, *The Great Depression, America 1929–1941* (New York: NY Times Books, 1984).

For Roosevelt's experiences during World War II, one might begin with James McGregor Burns, *Roosevelt: The Soldier of Freedom* (New York: Harcourt, Brace, Jovanovich, 1970). Other works include Robert Dallek, *Franklin D. Roosevelt and American Foreign Policy* (New York: Oxford University Press, 1981), Robert Divine, *Roosevelt and World War II* (New York: Penguin, 1971), Warren F. Kimball, *The Juggler: Franklin Roosevelt as Wartime Statesman* (Princeton, NJ: Princeton University Press, 1991), and Eric Larrabee, *Commander in Chief: Franklin Delano Roosevelt, His Lieutenants and Their War* (New York: Harper & Row, 1987).

The Internet can be an excellent source of information on Roosevelt if approached with some caution. By typing his name into a search engine, one will find thousands of potential Web sites to visit of quite varying quality. The most useful site probably is the Franklin D. Roosevelt Presidential Library and Museum site, at http://www.fdrlibrary.marist.edu, which offers access to online primary sources and images. One should also visit the New Deal Network site, at http://newdeal.feri.org. This site is the result of collaboration between the Franklin and Eleanor Roosevelt Institute, the Franklin D. Roosevelt Presidential Library, and Marist College. The site offers an impressive collection of documents, images, forums, and links regarding the United States during the Great Depression.

INDEX

About the Author

JEFFREY W. COKER is Assistant Professor of History at Belmont University. He is the author of *Confronting American Labor: The New Left Dilemma* (2002) and *Presidents from Taylor through Grant, 1849–1877: Debating the Issues in Pro and Con Primary Documents* (Greenwood, 2002)